Funny

Business

HARNESSING THE POWER OF PLAY
TO GIVE YOUR COMPANY A
COMPETITIVE ADVANTAGE

Funny
Business

CHRISTOPHER BYRNE

CAREER
PRESS
The Career Press, Inc.
Wayne, NJ

FUNNY BUSINESS
Edited by Jodi Brandon
Typeset by Eileen Munson
Cover design by Howard Grossman/12E Design
Printed in the U.S.A.

To order this title, please call toll-free 1-800-CAREER-1 (NJ and Canada: 201-848-0310) to order using VISA or MasterCard, or for further information on books from Career Press.

The Career Press, Inc.
220 West Parkway, Unit 12
Pompton Plains, NJ 07444
www.careerpress.com

Library of Congress Cataloging-in-Publication Data
CIP Data Available Upon Request.

~

For Michael G. Jackson,
and everyone who has used the power of play
to create their lives.

~

Contents

Introduction 9

Chapter 1: Defining Play 21

Chapter 2: Story—The Center of All Play 43

Chapter 3: Play vs. Recreation 73

Chapter 4: The Power of Playing Alone 81

Chapter 5: The Benefits of Group Play 103

Chapter 6: Boys and Girls Play Differently 129

Chapter 7: Play Is Assessing Information, Taking Risks, ...139
            and Taking Action

Chapter 8: Drop It if It Doesn't Work 173

Chapter 9: Playing the Game 185

Chapter 10: Get Playing 195

Acknowledgments 211

Index 213

About the Author 221

Introduction

There is perhaps no children's story sadder than that in Peter Pan. Originally the character of a play by James M. Barrie, today Peter is largely a beloved character seen as entertainment for children, mostly known these days from the classic Disney film or the musical starring Mary Martin that most Boomers grew up with. Peter is the boy who doesn't grow up, what Shakespeare called "boy eternal," and who lives in a world filled with freedom and adventure, where there is nothing to do all day but play, be with friends, and have none of the responsibilities of adulthood that, to him, seem oppressive.

But Barrie wasn't really talking about kids when he wrote the play. He had more serious issues in mind. The inspiration for the Peter Pan story was the death of Barrie's older brother in an ice-skating accident just before his 14th birthday. His mother's grief preserved an idealized memory of her son as a child and one who would never grow up. Barrie's anger and frustration at losing both a brother and, to some extent, a mother drove many of his creative efforts. Peter emerges as selfish and domineering, and his tragic flaw, to speak in literary terms, is that in order to stay young Peter has to forget his adventures. And thus, he is shut off from the world's best teacher: experience. His freedom, or what he considers freedom, ultimately comes at a price—that he must always experience the world as a child, divorced from the natural progression of life. He and his friends in Neverland are indeed lost boys, and that's not necessarily a good thing. The cost of eternal youth is that Peter will not—cannot—take his own place in the world as an integrated, mature human being. Peter is destined to be left behind always. Worse yet, he is stuck with a child's understanding and experience of the world, one that can never grow. Through Peter, we see—hopefully—that what we wish for is limited and ultimately bordering on the horrific. Peter is doomed to what, at least to me, is a horrid fate: never to change, never to live fully. More importantly, he is unable to access his accumulated experience in order to make better, more satisfying, and productive choices in his life.

All of this brings me to the fundamental question that was the impetus for this book: Is there a way to—sorry to be overly trite—have it all? Can we have the privileges and excitement of being an adult and the joy and freedom of childhood?

I believe we can. We need to rediscover how to play.

Now, I'm not saying to chuck everything and sit on the floor and play LEGOs all the time, lose days in video games, or ride bikes around the neighborhood. Just as play changes at different stages of children's development, it has relevance to adult lives as well. *Play* has become a dirty word for adults; it is synonymous with the frivolous, the pointless, the non-productive. Yet anyone who really understands the role that play has in the life of children will understand that it is none of those things. Play serves three essential functions: It allows new experiences. It fosters exploration. It facilitates expression. These are critical for each of us as individual humans, but they also allow us to be more effective in every aspect of our lives, including work.

In other words, to foster innovation, effective and productive work, better interpersonal skills, and greater satisfaction, we need to play. As we'll see, play in this context has a specific definition. It is not recreation or avoidance. Rather, play, as we'll define it here, provides an opening to engage more fully in everything we do and ultimately be more productive.

Learning to play is one of the most important things we do as children, but we do it naturally and associate it with pleasure, and therefore it doesn't seem like work. There's a popular cliché among children's experts that casts play as the work of children. However, I challenge that because it sets the two up as diametrically opposite; I suggest they are no such thing, that play and work are essentially the same. You could say work is the play of adults, or I'm suggesting you might give it a try.

Consider this: Both play and work are objective-driven and task-oriented. They have narratives, have conflicts, require ongoing problem solving, are seldom linear, have specific processes, are prone to interruption, thrive on disequilibration (much more on what that is and how it shapes so much of life to come), and are ultimately reflections of the individual(s) involved. The only difference is that we believe that play is fun and that work is not. Or should not be.

So how did we get to this point where "work" is onerous and "play," if you accept my premise that they share many of the same elements, is not? The answer is that it is cultural. And it goes back to the Bible (1 Corinthians 13:11): "When I was a child, I spoke like a child, I thought like a child, I reasoned like a child. When I became a man, I gave up childish ways." Perhaps even further. Every culture has its rites and traditions of passing from childhood into adulthood. But like any good thing, when it's taken to an extreme it can become problematic.

Yet a childhood that is largely leisure-based and protected from the adult world is a relatively new phenomenon. Whether in an agrarian or industrial world, child labor was essential, both as extra hands and to do things adults could not. Despite the work of reformers, writers, and pamphleteers, notably Charles Dickens, Coleridge, and others, children were essential to such industries as mining, chimney sweeping, furniture building, textile production. and many more, just in Britain alone. With the institution of mandatory public education, which goes back only to the mid-19th century, machines that could do the work of small hands, and a growing understanding of the health impacts of child labor, more and more children were liberated from working. Fast-forward to the 20th century, and what we call modern adolescence really began to take shape after the First World War and blossomed after the Second. Thus, the idea of childhood and youth as a carefree time without responsibility and the ability to indulge in play became part of today's culture. It is seen as a right of children. The prevailing attitude is: Life is going to be hard enough; let them enjoy being children. (As so often happens, there are many who think that because something has been true in their lifetime—and potentially their parents'—it has always been thus. That's just the way people are.) And so the idea of childhood as a time of freedom without responsibility, with security, and without serious or long-lasting consequences for one's actions was born. Buried, not so deeply, in this is the notion that adulthood is challenging, difficult, and unpleasant, so it's a kindness to shield kids from it as long as possible. And that's what we do today, to a certain extent in the United States. Before moving on from this, it must be noted that this is a particular phenomenon of the developed and comparatively affluent cultures. There are still parts of the world where children work and assume adult responsibilities from a very early age.

But back in the more privileged world, we have the oft-observed attitude that work is difficult and unpleasant, but it's necessary to make money, to provide for one's family and one's retirement—to shoulder all the responsibilities that Peter Pan so dreaded. The cost of having a good life and providing a good life for our families is the giving up of pleasure on a daily basis and finding it only in escape, whatever that is.

To understand a bit of how that has come about, we need to take a quick glance back at the development of business since World War II. (It's not that this is definitively the actual beginning of these trends, but for our purposes, that's far enough.) In the years following the war and as the United States prospered, military-style management was the norm. Simply put, orders were conveyed from up top and people fell into step. Workers did what they were told and were paid in return. As long as they stayed in line, they had job security, and if they demonstrated their ability, got to move up in the hierarchy to be the ones calling the shots. In the years after the war and for those who had survived the Great Depression, security was everything. The desire for that security, predictability, and stability was so important to so many that it trumped other desires. The father—for it was largely men at the time—provided for the family, ensured their lifestyle, and was the family hero. The "responsible adult" became not merely the norm but the ideal, as expressed in much popular entertainment during the Eisenhower years.

And it worked very well. The ability to provide was hugely important to those who had known deprivation and whose parents often, through no fault of their own, had not been able to. If the period is remembered as one of staid conventionality and adherence to cultural norms that were restrictive, it's important to remember that that is seen through the filter of our current experience and ideas. Some compassion toward the people and their time is required.

I still vividly remember our Jewish neighbor in the suburban development we lived in (with the glorious post-war name of "Holiday Hills") talking with my parents on our front lawn. He and his wife had lived in Germany as the war broke out, and their families had managed to get out of the country just in advance of Hitler. I still remember him saying, "You can't imagine what it feels like to have the children running up and down the street yelling, 'Come see our sukkah!'" If freedom had a cost and that cost was the loss of individual expression and an adherence to cultural norms, then millions were willing to pay it. That, of course, reinforced the system and became for that generation "the way things were done." Fear of instability and protecting kids from experiencing what they had was a tremendous motivator for many adults.

As in so many other ways, Baby Boomers, the children of these stability- and security-seekers, would totally upend this structure, and the world would change dramatically. As Feste says in *Twelfth Night*, "the whirlygig of time brings in its revenges." And those would be seismic.

The downside of the adult seeking to provide security, despite whatever costs to him or her individually, would echo down the next generation and completely transform the culture, yet again. The military model didn't just appear in business: It appeared in many families as well. Although children had new freedoms, had security, and benefitted richly from parents' desire to provide the things that they had not had, the archetypal family of the period was led by the father, who was often removed from the lives of the kids, and "youth culture" began to emerge as separate from adults, with its own music, entertainment, toys, and so forth. Add to this the mobility of the post-war years, and the family changed. Multiple generations did not share a town or a roof as much, and it became the norm to go where the opportunity was. This began to create a generational divide that had previously been unknown.

And then came Vietnam. Or, rather, then came the draft for the Vietnam conflict. The generation that had been raised to think for themselves was the first to question *en masse* the wisdom of the military model. They would not just fall into step. This is, I know, a gross simplification, and much has been written about this. I mention it here only to show the generational shift that would impact all aspects of the culture moving forward and that would challenge—and ultimately transform—the established status quo.

Where it impacted business is that the workforce was the most educated it had ever been, and these empowered people in many instances wanted more fulfillment from their work. Women were beginning to make deeper and deeper inroads into the corporate world, and cultures were changing. The children who had felt distanced from their parents determined that they would be friends to their children and, like every generation before them, were not going to make the "same mistakes" their parents had. And the era of self-realization and finding fulfillment as a result of one's work began. It was yet another change, and the economy and markets began to expand. This, in turn, gave rise to a period of opportunity and optimism that created the spirit of the 1980s and the sense that everything was going to keep going up. (Humans are particularly myopic in this way. We tend to think that anything that has been going on for two or three years represents "the way it's always been." And we are particularly likely to do that when the way it is rewards us.) The longer view of history, of course, shows us that everything is cyclical, and the next turning of time's whirlygig would set the stage for what we see today.

Three events subsequently reshaped the economy and the culture and set up the current situation: the stock market crash of 1987, the dotcom bubble, and the housing collapse of 2008. (Economists, I know that this is a gross simplification and condensation.)

Put simply, people got scared. As markets became saturated with product and segments matured, the general zeitgeist dictated "Hold on to what you have." "Be careful." "Look for the sure thing." Of course, there have been breakout hits in recent years, and of course some investors have done very well, but aside from consumer electronics (and not even that across the board), playing it safe has been the watchword. Having been scared, the natural inclination is to protect what you have—to hold tighter.

Just look at the auto industry. From the '50s onward, the new model years were a national event, and families would visit dealerships as an outing merely to see the new introductions. American automobiles represented unique innovation worldwide. Today, the auto industry, like many other industries, is global, and there has been little innovation besides the addition of bells and whistles—mostly technology-driven— in the past decade or more. To understand this, one only need to look at toys and play, which are always a reflection of the larger culture. In the 1970s, kids loved muscle cars and collected Hot Wheels. They were cool and fast, and created the imaginary experience of driving fast, taking risks, and being larger than life. Today, what do we see? Luxury and comfort. I ask you: When was the last time you saw a 5-year-old want to play "luxury and comfort"?

And I see this in all kinds of consumer goods. The goal is not to innovate; it's to survive. That's not invalid, obviously. The first rule of every organism is survival. (And though I don't consider companies people, I do consider them organisms in an abstract way.) But at what cost? In consumer products, that means one or two leaders and a lot of other attempts to ride those coattails. The same can be said of movies, at least to a certain extent. Formulaic, nearly identical movies are released one after another. And whenever there is a breakout hit, the imitators rush in. The results are blandness and battles for market share, and more importantly short-term thinking, the need to get through the next quarter, not lose one's job, play it safe. These may be necessary, of course, but they don't drive innovation or creativity—or make people particularly happy in their jobs.

What causes this? Partially it's fear. From product development to hiring to management practice to even how children play, risk management is the overriding issue. People are scared of trying something new. Every action is calculated not to maximize opportunity but to mitigate risk. Of course, there are many other factors inhibiting innovation, from short-term thinking to a need for immediate results for a month end or a quarter or a year. These all end up having the effect of companies kicking the can down the road, and individual professionals hope that they'll be on to the next job before the chickens come home to roost and the shit hits the fan. (Loading sentences with clichés can be so amusing.) Levity aside, the creative process can often take longer than a quarter or a year, and boards and executives get scared of investing that, especially when Wall Street is watching.

The problem with fear, short-term thinking, and going for the next quarter's numbers is that ultimately it is unsustainable. It is not a business strategy; it is a survival mechanism, and we see it way too much in contemporary business.

One quick example before we jump deeper into a possible way out. At this writing, we are just past the holiday shopping season in 2014. It was, at best, lackluster. There were no products—aside from a few electronics—that people were talking about. Consumers concerned about overspending kept their wallets shut. Did it pick up in the last weeks of the season? A bit. But the cycle is likely to repeat in 2015 and beyond because there is a wholly new consumer out there, one that has been created by the very businesses who are hoping to get them racing to the stores to buy. This consumer has been conditioned to wait for sales and has nothing new that he or she "needs" to buy. Even having specific products in hand by Christmas holiday has become less important with the rise of the gift card. The balance of power has shifted—from consumers being targeted with the newest, the latest, the hottest, and so forth, to consumers being in control of when they buy and, in some cases, when they spend. The world has changed, and many companies are still doing things the old way.

To get out of this situation requires a new way of thinking. It requires new ways of creating products, determining profitability, reaching consumers, and building businesses. Obviously, every business has its own specific challenges and opportunities. However, in this new market, new ways of doing business are required.

So how do we get there?

Well, by taking a cue from kids. That is, we can play our way there.

And that's what this book is all about: how the principles of play can be used to foster an innovative culture. We'll start with a look at play, what it really is, and how it can be used to change thinking and ultimately be transformative. We can start with remembering that every great idea began as something from the imagination. We'll then look at the different elements of play and how each of those can be used individually and in the context of a business.

This book was inspired by consulting with individuals and companies that I've done over the years designed to foster creativity and new solutions to old problems. It dawned on me over time, particularly because so much of my work has been in the toy business, that what we were really asking people to do was play. I encountered many adults who felt that play was something for kids and that it had no place in their lives. (We'll get into the difference between play and recreation in our next chapter.) Yet, when they saw the power of play and began to tap into the imagination they thought they had to leave behind, some positive change began to happen.

Given all of this, one might think that adults might play more. But here it's necessary to make an important distinction: There is a big difference between play as we will define it and leisure activity. In fact, they may be diametrically opposed. Whereas leisure activity is an escape, play is a process of deep immersion, as we hope will become clear in the following pages.

Many of the stories I've included here were told in confidence, and so although I don't identify companies or individuals, the situations are real. Some of these have been resolved and some, as we'll see, are still in process at this writing. We're not sure where they're going—and that's part of the play process as well.

The good news is that, unlike Peter Pan, we can remember our past adventures, and while not being bound by them, each of us already has a wealth of knowledge and experience to draw from. How that works will become clear in short order. For now, though, let's get playing.

Defining Play

Play, in its simplest terms, begins with asking the question "What if?"

For a child, it's asking, "What if I stack these blocks as high as I can?" or "What if my Teenage Mutant Ninja Turtles figures stomp on the bad guys?"

The idea takes shape in the mind, and the child, in this case, puts it into action and sees where it takes him or her. And therein lies the key.

Play is really nothing more than an idea followed by action where the outcome is not known until the action is taken. Now, you might say that this is like a science experiment, and in a way it is. Experiments, though, are devised out of a desire to prove or disprove a hypothesis. Play, on the other hand, starts not with a hypothesis but an idea inspired in the moment.

With respect to the above children's play situations, the answer to the "What If?" question might be a stack of four bricks. Perhaps eight. Perhaps a story of total annihilation of the bad guys takes shape. Perhaps one is captured and converted to being a good guy. That outcome, that moment of play, will inevitably lead to the next question and the next action until it's time to pick up the toys or go to bed or do homework or whatever the next thing in the child's life is.

For children, play serves three essential developmental functions: It provides new experiences. It allows them to explore their worlds. And it allows them to express themselves. Over time what kids discover and learn about themselves and their culture will create the experiences that help shape their personalities and their perceptions of the world. It will allow them to locate themselves as individuals within the context of their peers and their families. It will give them a chance to try on different responses to situations and to discover themselves—all within the relatively safe confines of childhood. Play is both profound in terms of how it shapes our realities and cumulative in that its true impact on a developing personality is only realized over time. Play, as many have said, is rehearsal for adulthood, and as a tool of learning and socialization, it is more complex than simply asking a question and getting an answer, but that's a good place to start for our purposes.

(As a side note, what I've described previously is generally referred to as "open-ended play." It is centered on the imagination and what is created out of it. It's distinct from directed play in which there is a specific objective [i.e., complete the LEGO model].)

So, why should this be bad thing for adults—and not a lifelong habit? Probably because play has gotten a bad name in our culture, largely because it is associated with childhood and immaturity. In fact, for adults, *play* is considered a bad word. It evokes a lack of seriousness. It is seen as aimless, unproductive, and wasteful. To say someone is playing is tantamount to saying that they're not contributing effectively—that, somehow, they are not really adults.

I blame St. Paul. Seriously.

In 1 Corinthians 13:11, Paul threw an effective wet blanket on play that has endured nearly 2,000 years. He wrote, "When I was a child, I talked like a child. I thought like a child. I reasoned like a child, but when I became a man I put away childish things."

Gee, thanks. This has been used for millennia to quash the creative spirit. (I'm exaggerating for effect, but only a little.) So for many cultures, play became one of those childish things that were to be put away. After a certain age there were to be no more flights of fancy. No more pretending to be a superhero. No spending the afternoon staring at clouds, building forts, and so forth. Life for adults was serious business, and anything that smacked of childishness had to be banished.

This is seriously misguided, however, because play is serious business.

And play belongs in business because it is the catalyst that leads to innovation, and that is sorely needed in today's competitive economy. If you accept the definition of play provided earlier, then you know that the concept of play is really about releasing the creative force within each of us, to affect our lives. Just as a child might make up a story about Spider Man, we make up the stories of our lives.

You make it up. You make it *all* up. You really do.

Ideally, how we live our lives is play in its purest form, and it is one of the most powerful things we can do for ourselves and for businesses. We do it every day, whether we recognize it or not in our personal and professional lives—and, incidentally, I don't buy that work and personal lives can be separate; we are the same body, the same heart, mind, and soul, whether we're sitting at our desks or in our homes. We are professionals and consumers—and we are powerful individuals who, if we're willing, can use play to transform our lives and our businesses.

So why limit yourself because you think something should be a certain way? In fact, the notion of what it means to be a "grown-up" and not to play is something that was made up.

It's the darker side of what Kermit the Frog songs about in "The Rainbow Connection": "Somebody thought of it/And someone believed it. Look what it's done so far."

Everything we know and believe starts as an idea, something created in the imagination—from the religions of the world to Apple computer. The essential component, though, is the belief in the potential reality of what you've made up. It is to see and embrace possibility. This is the catalyst for action. It is a form of practical wizardry. And, yes, people can be wizards—*are* wizards. That's right: You're no different from Harry Potter and his friends. Fictional wizards use words with the expectation of making something happen. Leave out the wands, capes, and mystical creatures, and by another name that's a business plan. (You'll never think of PowerPoint the same way again.) On its most elemental level, your words—and time—create a new reality when put into action, and you create something that hadn't existed before you cast your spell. Just as a child might get his or her friends to build a fort or a sand castle, so does a manager get all his or her employees to build a great product. It's really no different. Something that didn't exist through the power of imagination, words, belief, and action becomes real. Thus, what grown-ups call strategic planning by any other name is its own kind of magic, though any marketing strategist would probably stab him- or herself before admitting that. Too bad.

You Don't Grow Out of Play! But You Might Grow Into It.

If you take anything away from the foregoing, it should be that play isn't something you leave behind you when you get older. Rather, it should be an essential part of your toolkit, something you can access when needed.

But, obviously, there is a difference between the way adults play and the way kids do, just by virtue of cognitive development and experience.

Before we get into the way adults can play productively and effectively, however, let's take a step back and understand in a little more detail the importance of play in overall child development.

There is plenty of scholarly research on play, and you can study people like Piaget, Montessori, and many others. However, what they'll tell you is in the context of child development and what children learn at different stages, and we're dealing with people who are already developed (however you might think of some of your co-workers).

Whatever theory of play you subscribe to—or none for that matter—they all basically talk about the same thing: how children learn to be in the world. There are the cognitive elements related to learning and the accumulation of experiences that allow for some level of predictability and then, of course, the social aspects of learning to function in relation to other people. By the time we get to be adults, we forget what hard work this is for children for several reasons. We have internalized the lessons and they've become a part of us, and we don't give them a second thought.

Probably the best example of this is learning to ride a bike. Think back to the struggle of balancing on two wheels and pedaling. It is not something that comes naturally to us as humans. Remember how many times you teetered and fell off, and ultimately that moment when everything came together and your body adapted to it. (Older folks may have more recent memories of adapting to bifocals or progressive lenses.) Most likely that stunt of balancing and pedaling is something you couldn't *un*learn, no matter how hard you tried. It's the same thing with virtually every play experience you had as a child. You are actually building synapses based on physical or cognitive experiences that didn't just become esoteric knowledge: They became part of your body. What dancers refer to as "muscle memory" really is how we've learned. (And, as we'll see later, why it's so difficult for many people to change courses.)

I'll give you one more example that's so commonplace as to be almost trite, but it's something I hear all the time from adults. The conversation usually begins with something like this: "We gave little Snookums this wonderful toy, and he only played with the box."

Generally that's used as a way to express disappointment that an expensive item went disregarded as the child's attention is captivated by something that is considered disposable. And the conversation stops there. But there's something important in this that has direct relevance to effective management in the adult, business world as well.

Why does the child play with the box and not the toy? That usually happens because the toy is too sophisticated, complicated, or involved for the child's level of development. When things are too confusing, children don't engage with them, not out of disinterest, but because they can't. They haven't developed to the point where they can. It's that simple. The box, on the other hand, has direct relevance to what they already know: working the flaps, putting things in and taking them out, picking it up and putting it on their heads. This is fun! And it's fun largely because it starts out being familiar but there are cool things to discover along the way. It's important to note that what looks like repetitive activity by the child is actually creating and reinforcing neural pathways in the child's brain with each repetition.

Watching a child abandon a toy that he or she has no interest in is often frustrating for an adult because the adult thinks the child *should* be able to do that. We hear all the time things along the lines of "This toy is designed for kids ages 6 and up, but little precious is so bright that at 4 he can handle it." Well, he can't. Because even an advanced 4-year-old doesn't yet have the brain development of a 6-year-old. It can't happen. The pitfall is that as adults unless we consciously try we can't conceive of how a child perceives things.

We also see this a lot with respect to technology. "My little one can work the iPad!" parents crow with great pride. To an extent, yes, he or she can. However, I highly recommend thinking about what is actually happening when the iPad is being "worked." It's not like the little tyke can manage a bank account from the touchscreen. Rather, he or she is doing something rudimentary that even a child of a year can do: touch something and observe a reaction. This is a fundamental element of infant play. It's not different from putting a spoon in a pot. That's actually an important part of infant play because each time the child engages in the action, he or she is learning something new—perceiving something new. Touching an icon and watching an app open up is no different.

This has application throughout life as we try to learn new things. Quite frankly, unless we're naturally talented, we're going to suck at anything new when we first start out. But over time, and with practice and attention, we get better at it. Sure, natural talent may make the difference between mere competence and exceptional performance, but it's the experience that counts. As Steve Jobs reportedly said, it takes about 10,000 hours of practice to become an expert at something. Obviously, that's a statement open to debate and probably said as much for its value as a sound bite as truth. But the point is, you have to work at something to be good at it—at least for something that doesn't come naturally.

Yes, we hear all sorts of stuff about how people get "too old" to do new things, but brain science doesn't bear that out. It may take you a little longer to build synapses as your body chemistry changes, but it can still happen. Rather, what I consistently observe is that change is threatening, and if people are doing okay, then they don't want to invest the effort. But, as we all know, in a competitive business environment, "doing okay" isn't going to cut it in the long run.

When I was first starting out, I had an older colleague who told me that his career strategy was "keep my head down and not get cut." He was actually a great guy who achieved a middling level of success (in my opinion). Though his career strategy served him for a couple of decades, he ultimately found himself in his early 50s getting cut and struggling to find work. His ability to survive in a corporate setting was not an accomplishment that most companies were looking to hire.

Play is the antithesis of this kind of sedentary career goal. It's about always looking for what's new and next, trying it out, and seeing where it takes you. It's about opening up to what's possible and being willing to let experience teach you without being hobbled by fear. To me, at least, that's a much more fun way to live anyway.

Why Play Works—And Why Other Things Might Not

This is why what we're calling play needs to become part of your daily consciousness and practice. Play works because it is organically human. It comes naturally to us as mammals, and it is in our nature. It doesn't need to be learned. It keeps us involved and engaged in life and seeking new experiences.

On some level you could say it's a semantic argument, that what I'm talking about is just another way of saying "best practices," and that, as grown-ups, what I'm calling play is just another name for learning. I'll get to why it's different in a moment.

There is a whole—highly profitable—industry out there designed to make you a better, more effective, and more successful person. You can read countless other books and attend seminars on being more creative, unleashing whatever is leashed up inside you that's holding you back from success, and so on and so on.

If you've tried these things, ask: Have they worked? Are you more successful, prosperous, or advanced in your career because of this stuff? Have you made more money, achieved your goals? Have you tipped? Do you practice the habits that have made you the powerhouse you always dreamed of being? Have you become adept at putting the big rocks in the box first? All of these have been suggested as key steppingstones in achieving wealth, success, fame, power, and a private jet. (It kind of sounds like a game show when you put it that way, doesn't it?)

If these have worked for you, congratulations. I applaud you for time and money well spent and your diligence as a student. Of course, I also wonder why you're now reading this, but maybe you're a perpetual seeker.

For most people, though, these systems, methodologies, and so forth don't work the way they hoped they would. And they don't work for one very specific reason: They are not natural. Yes, they sound good, and they seem to lay out a roadmap that anyone can follow, and so we believe it and buy the book or go the seminar, and we diligently try for a week or two or three to put these new practices into play, but ultimately, without a systemic, cultural change in a workplace that supports this kind of wholesale change, most people inevitably go back to their own way of doing things. That's completely predictable because that's our nature. We don't change until not changing is more painful or difficult than changing, as any psychologist will tell you. And, as we'll see in a bit, change doesn't happen in a vacuum.

Now, I'm not discounting all these other methods, their solutions, learning and adopting new practices to be more effective—not at all. They all have some very helpful insights, but what I am saying is that a wholesale change in character based on a book or a seminar is not possible. All of these systems seem to provide answers by imposing information on us. Play, on the other hand, comes from within. It is organic and as individual as each of us is.

If you watch children play, you can see that each has a different play style. I was really kinetic and loved running around and jumping. I loved things that engaged my gross motor skills and loved to ride my bike, climb trees, and be in motion. My older brother was quieter and less likely to run around like a hooligan. His idea of fun was poring over baseball statistics. But we both recall our summers as fun because we were doing what came naturally to us as individuals. Your play style never changes. It is an essential part of your personality, and determining and acknowledging it are critical because that determines how you approach virtually every challenge. Even as adults, my brother and I still approach things pretty much the same as we did when we were kids, though I'm not breaking as many things around the house these days, and I haven't broken a bone in decades. So, a single, prescriptive methodology for how we are supposed to work is not going to be effective for both of us. We simply aren't going to do things that are imposed on us and at odds with our individual play style. We'll talk more about how play styles and effective management come together later.

First, though, we need to examine why we rush toward these all-encompassing "solutions" again and again Well, it's also part of human nature. If it's not literally part of our DNA, as the need to play is, it is still culturally ingrained over centuries. Just look back at advertising, fads, and what-have-you. From tulips to Beanie Babies, there was always something that could make you rich. From Dale Carnegie to Sheryl Sandberg, there was always a way to be more successful. Essentially, though, these things kill play because they try to force people into boxes or ways of thinking or being that may inhibit rather than empower them. We allow children to be who they are, always within a structure; why do we not allow adults to do the same?

One reason is that we always buy into an external idea of success, or at least think we should. Success in the adult world is often defined as money, power, and prestige. Essentially, we buy into cultural benchmarks that stifle our desire to make it up. We end up playing someone else's game, to put it in the terms of play. Success—or rather finding the "guaranteed" path to success—is as much a fashion as hemlines or hairstyles. As a culture, we are always looking for the "magic bullet" that will solve all our problems. We want to win the lottery. We're going to invent the killer app, and so forth. We idolize the stars who seem to defy the odds and become hugely successful, and try to imitate what they do. There is a level of magical thinking that accompanies all of this, or at least a lot of imagination into foreseeing a different future.

That's important because, as we've said, all change begins in the imagination. But given your unique play style and the realities of your life, it boils down to the actions you take. Of course, the problem is that it's never possible to control for all the variables not accounted for in these self-help, transformative methodologies, and the biggest variable is each of us as individuals. That doesn't stop us from trying to take in the lessons of these people who have been successful—nor should it. Many of these people have great ideas and important lessons to teach. The problems arise when companies try to implement things because they are the current hot topic, rather than extracting the lessons, doing an analysis, and applying them to the situation at hand. But there is not going to be one solution that works for everyone.

I had a client in the '90s who insisted that everyone he worked with use a certain day planner system. This wasn't just a calendar; it was marketed as an essential tool for success with great sayings from important people who were supposed to inspire us every time we made a dentist appointment, or some such. This client was messianic about this system, and woe be to the person on the business who didn't show up with their planner to meetings.

Of course, the problem was that for anyone who wasn't wired to respond to this kind of organizational process, who didn't have time or patience to delve into the more esoteric nature of this system, the calendar was just a calendar.

Fashion dictates that we all run like a herd toward something without really thinking.

Without the appropriate application of theories and methodologies to a unique situation, these hot management solutions become the Birkin bag of business. Stay with me here for a moment. The Birkin bag was created by Hermès in the early 1980s. It's a capacious, custom-made bag, and its sheer expense (high five figures and up) make it a symbol of status and success. It is much admired and much sought after, but its size makes it somewhat impractical for many people. Still, "having" it is more important than its utility—at least for several women who have described acquiring one to me with quiet ecstasy and sure that it would elevate them in my eyes.

So, the flaw with these fashionable management practices is that without specific application to the tasks at hand, they can become extremely expensive and not very practical. Moreover, they can be huge time wasters.

Several years ago, I was hired by a company to consult on how to make their product "tip." The president of this privately held company had read Malcolm Gladwell's *The Tipping Point* and became convinced that all he needed to do was to make his product "tip," and the profits would materialize out of thin air. Now, I'm a fan of Gladwell's book, and it makes great reading, but it's more a sociological study than a roadmap for success. In each of the cases Gladwell cites, he has the advantage of hindsight, and there is always at least one element that couldn't have been planned for. Sorry, that's not replicable; it's often just luck. You can set the stage with solid planning and an effective marketing plan that you think will work, but setting your goal at "tipping" in the Gladwell sense is like playing the lottery. It may happen, but is that worth staking your business on?

The other thing about fashions is that they change. In the case of management practices, the failure of the new idea over time to create transformative change means it's abandoned and things go back to "normal" until the next thing comes along. And it will. There is nothing wrong with a fashion, or even a fashionable idea. The downside, however, is that they can be distracting, take you away from your central objectives, and ultimately be costly. It's important to ask: What are you buying into now because it's a hot topic, and are you willing to do the analysis to determine its viability to your unique situation? To put it in the terms of play, think back to when you told your mom, "But *everyone* is doing it!" What did she say? Probably something like, "If everyone told you to jump off a bridge, would you do that?" Seriously, things don't change that much as we get older.

This brings up the reason why my client who wanted to make his product tip—and many like him—latch onto these so-called solutions: They have been effectively marketed. Potential customers have been convinced that a product or an idea answers a perceived need. Reach enough people who have a perceived need often enough with your message, and you'll likely make sufficient sales to keep you in the black. My client needed to increase revenues significantly in a short period of time. Gladwell's study of fads seemed to provide an answer: Just find the right people to talk about it, and—presto—you're a major hit. Ultimately, Gladwell's study is more fascinating as sociology than management practice. Moreover, everything that tipped in his book has subsequently toppled, and in the natural course of time, the market has changed and moved on. The idea of tipping as a panacea and an easy solution may not have been what Gladwell intended, but it's what a significant part of the market believed, and it drove huge sales to people looking for the solution. For the publisher and Gladwell, it was the very definition of "all's fish that comes to my net." And good for them.

To the marketer, his or her job ends when the customer makes the purchase. How the customer got there is an ongoing process of manipulation. Set up a problem. Create a need. Offer the solution. I always think of the character Mary Sunshine from the musical *Chicago*. She says, "They'll fall for it hook, line, and sinker because it's what they want." Pretty much all marketing through the ages can be reduced to that sentence.

In the 1980s, I wrote infomercials for fitness equipment. The stuff was crap. It was cheaply produced, of questionable effectiveness, and very expensive for what it was. We sold tonnage. The combination of adequate production values, fitness celebrities, and the dream that minimal investment would yield maximum results, worked. Thirty years later that dream is still alive—and still selling lots of products.

Don't get me wrong. I love marketing. I think it's absolutely fascinating to determine what will make people want to buy a product and then get them to. But when it comes to potentially buying into new management practices (or a new car, for that matter), I would encourage a bit more play. Just as a child picks up a rock to see what's underneath, the play in this case comes from delving more deeply into the subject matter. Why do children take things apart? Because they're naturally curious and want to learn how things work. Adults may call it analysis, but it's the same premise. The problem arises when we don't take the time to take things apart, understand how they work, and see if the actual effectiveness of something supports the emotional response that might make the sale.

This brings us to our third—and arguably most important—element of selling: catharsis. Founded in the emotions, it is the basis of all sales. By definition, catharsis is the release of pent-up emotion, and that can be expressed in narrative as in the climax of a story, or in the purchase of something that would seem to resolve some kind of emotional conflict.

In human terms, catharsis is essential. It always marks a turning point in a life. But catharsis is short-lived, and what matters are the actions taken after the catharsis. Because of fashion and marketing, it's easy to get swept along on a tide of emotion. In business, though, we're supposed to abjure emotion. Business, at least, is supposed to be the alpha and omega of rationality in a world run mad with emotion, to speak in the language of movie trailers.

In reality, complete rationality is hardly ever true. More decisions are made based on emotion and gut feeling than we might like to admit. Oh, sure, we can build rational defenses to support our choices, but at the end of the day, there is always a level of emotion in any choice we make. This is not a bad thing. It's a natural human tendency. So, hooray for catharsis; it proves we're alive. Now, what are you going to do with it?

Most people know Tony Robbins, management guru, celebrity, and extraordinary showman. I had a client who wanted to change how the agency worked both internally and with clients. So, the transformation promised by Robbins's seminars seemed like the answer. (This was after several productivity and organizational experts had gone through the agency and given their best shot.) All of us trotted off for two days in the expensive seats down front, and the experience was nothing short of amazing. Robbins is dynamic, and the information is very practical, and even things that one could actually do. The experience is part lecture, part Broadway show, and when an entire auditorium has leapt to its feet cheering over enhancing personal and organizational productivity, you know you've got a cathartic experience on your hands. And therein lies the rub. It's not that Robbins's methods don't work, and it's not that people didn't leave charged up about changing their lives; they certainly did. The problem arises when the culture around that empowerment doesn't change. To give Robbins his due, he talks about systemic change and offers tools, but the catharsis he creates has to be followed by action, and that's not his job. (His job is done when the horse is led to the water, so to speak, unless you hire him as an ongoing consultant.)

A week after this event, people at the agency were still buzzing about how much "fun" it had been. One afternoon, I was sitting with the president of the agency, who had not participated, by the way, and asked what he was going to do to change internal practices to accommodate his newly energized team—to capitalize on the catharsis, as it were. He looked at me like I had two heads. It had never crossed his mind that the experience alone was not enough. In fact, there was no structural or cultural change in the agency, and within another week when the rosy glow had well and truly worn off, things were back to "normal," and it was as if this had never happened. Catharsis, then, without lasting change, is wasted.

The problem with all of these practices is not, as noted previously, that they are inherently flawed but the application of them is not consistent with how humans are. Wholesale change is not possible, just as the peak, cathartic experience is not sustainable. Lasting change is slow. Just ask anyone who has successfully lost weight. We humans with our short lives and immediate needs, however, tend to believe that there is one answer when there are many.

That's why play works. First, it comes naturally to human beings. It doesn't have to be learned; it's infinitely adaptable to the unique personalities and perspective of the individuals involved, and it can complement virtually any other practice. It is not about finding *one* answer but about trying different things until one works. It's about using what's at hand and being open to changing directions.

Embracing the Process

It bears repeating that when children play, they are practicing being human beings. They try on roles and explore different scenarios. But they are also doing something significantly more important: They are building those learning experiences that will help them in the future. Whether blocks, or LEGOs, or running around like hooligans, play is the foundation for all learning, whether intellectual or experiential.

Think of it this way: When a child is building a stack of blocks, he or she is doing so much more than just piling them up. He or she is getting firsthand experience in problem-solving, the ability to see a solution, and even rudimentary physics. Learning is kinesthetic through trial and error. Yet so is most human knowledge. Being able to apply knowledge through the process of asking "What if?" is the basis for all innovation and creativity.

In high school, I was an indifferent math student at best. One of my best teachers, however, was my 10th-grade geometry teacher. Her famous line was "Let's close our books and reason together." The whole idea was to use our imaginations to come up with ways to prove or disprove theorems using the information we had—and our imaginations.

Consider, for a moment, the arch as a component of architecture. The Gothic arch made it possible to have the huge open spaces of castles and cathedrals. Yet before that was discovered, there were millennia of different attempts to create buildings. The pointed Gothic arch, in comparison to some of the rudimentary constructions of earlier civilizations, when it appeared, was a high point in technological advancement. It was a slow and imperfect process driven by intuition and empirical evidence, which is a fancy way of saying play. The important thing to remember, though, is that without the inevitable failure that is part of play (e.g., the blocks fell down on repeated tries), we can't get to a successful solution. Knowledge grows out of the ability to re-create that solution, to codify it in equations and designs that allow others to replicate the success. Still, the play came first.

There are things that can be learned based on studying previous achievements, but there are also things that every child must experience directly in order to learn: eating, walking, riding a bike, stacking blocks, and so forth. And each child does it in his or her own time, though there are naturally occurring milestones that are generally constant from child to child within what are considered acceptable variations for normal development. As children develop, their play changes because they change and grow, and what they are able to do and understand is based on the development of the body and the brain. The myth is that once we hit adulthood, we stop growing and changing.

In my elementary school, I was almost a year younger than the oldest kid in the class. In fact, I was one of the youngest in my grade. This didn't really affect me with the academic work, but I was a disaster in gym class. Gym was a source of non-stop failure and frustration for me, amplified by ridicule and criticism from the teacher and my classmates. However, given that I was almost a year younger, there were things that I simply could not do as I hadn't developed sufficiently. In a perfect world, I would have taken gym class with the grade below me where what was being taught was consistent with my physical development. I won't go so far as to say "I coulda been a contender." Still, I would probably have been more successful had I been taught at the level of my physical development at that time.

By now, you surely see where this is going in terms of business and management. The part of play that is discovery and learning is essential to effective working and managing. As a manager, you need to be asking whether or not your team has the information and experience—the level of development, in other words—in order to be successful. As an employee, it means taking control of your own job functions and figuring out what the next move is—and failing from time to time.

This is critical, and we'll talk about it in more detail later, but the process of play is all about failure. The entrepreneurs I talk to and work with on a regular basis know this. They freely admit that if one in eight or 10 things they try turns into a profitable project or business, then they're well ahead of the curve. They also admit that they are constantly trying things, failing, trying again. So, what they have is an understanding of play in this context, and they have internalized a practice of framing "failure" as simply acquiring more information.

I have a friend who is a working actor on Broadway, on tours, and in the movies. He auditions for many, many more parts than he ever gets. He's even gotten parts and lost them as rehearsals have begun, but what he always says is "It was a chance to perform." And that's what drives him. It's not about winning the part as much having opportunities to express himself as an artist. Of course, he has to succeed sometimes or he wouldn't eat, but he also knows that a failure in one instance is nothing more than a momentary event or disappointment. The larger picture—the *overriding intention*—is stronger than the individual event. This is one of the things children know inherently. Going back to our illustration of stacking blocks, the falling down can be as entertaining as trying again with the information gathered from the collapse of the tower.

But here's the real catch and part of the cultural bias against play as we're discussing it here: You have to admit y*ou don't know.* This is one of the biggest inhibitors to play in our culture.

That's something that no one wants to admit to—especially in business. When I talk to managers about this subject, it's one that fills them with dread. They have bought into the belief that they're *supposed* to know and be able to guarantee results. A significant portion of their self-image is tied up in knowing. They believe that their power with and over other people comes from knowing. When I suggest they say "I don't know," they resist. It causes a great deal of stress because rather than admitting they don't know, they feel they have to appear to know something (anything) even if they don't, which in turn creates defensiveness when challenged, which—not surprisingly—puts the kibosh on creativity and innovation. We'll talk about the creative power of saying "I don't know" later on.

The corollary to "I don't know," at least in this case, is that I don't have the exact answer. Certainly not for you. I have an inbred resistance to prescriptive solutions for business problems. There is no one answer, and more importantly there's not even necessarily a "right" answer. What you have is a series of choices presented at different times. This mindset is the essence of play as we're discussing it here, and it takes the "right" and "wrong" out of the equation. There are actions, results, and results based on those actions.

In my own career, I'm consistently aware that I've made it up in just this way. There is no job description for what I do. However, there has been one phrase that has consistently guided my career, and it's one that is the ultimate definition of play: "Sure, I'll try that." And that is the essence of play.

I guess I should add that "I'll try that" is not a knee-jerk reaction. It's always advisable to assess the chances of success before jumping into something. When I was a kid and our goal was to jump from one garage roof to another in our neighborhood (which always upset our moms for some reason), we took into account the risk, but we did it anyway.

Reduced to its simplest elements, the process of play can be reduced to a series of statements and questions:

What's up?

What if…?

I don't know.

You want to find out?

Sure, what do you want to do?

Okay, let's try that.

How did that turn out?

You want to do that again?

What do you want to do now?

If you respond to each of these honestly and fearlessly, you'll be actively engaged in the play process—just like kids on a Saturday afternoon. Of course, I can hear all sorts of people sputtering, "It's not that simple." Well, it is. I would challenge you to look at anything you've done and see if these don't apply. Now, the key is honesty and fearlessness, and we'll get into that.

For now, I'd just like you to think about how this level of simplicity can, in fact, be liberating. One of the great things about play is that this process, as noted previously, can be applied to any practice or methodology. And for people who say to me, "I wish I could spend my days playing," my response is always, "You can."

Story—The Center of All Play

There is one common element of every human civilization, about as far back as we can tell. As a defining principle it is unsurpassed. As a method for organizing and motivating people, its effectiveness has been demonstrated over centuries. Even when ultimately proven wrong or displaced by something newer, the basic principle remains unchanged.

Of course, we're talking about stories.

Play is all about telling stories. Stories form the basis of beliefs, and beliefs dictate actions. This may seem like a gross simplification, but it is nonetheless true. Consider everyone's favorite holiday guy, Santa Claus. Belief in Santa has driven the toy industry for years. Approximately 70 percent of toy sales in the United States occur in the weeks leading up to Christmas. And it's not just kids. Belief in the need to give presents at Christmas plays a critical role in the overall retail business. And why? Because millions of people believe that giving presents is an essential and unavoidable—if sometimes frustrating—part of Christmas celebrations. But it wasn't always thus.

The early Puritans in the colonies outlawed Christmas celebrations. The story was that this was a somber occasion. In the 19th century both in the United States and Europe, the fashion was to give cards, and an entire industry grew up around that. At the dawn of the 20th century, retailers were desperate to shore up their business, which flagged in the fourth quarter. The story may be apocryphal, but R.H. Macy is often credited with creating the modern practice of giving presents. It certainly makes sense. At the time, the fourth quarter was deadly for sales, particularly when he was selling dry goods. It worked, and the modern retail calendar was born with an emphasis on Black Friday and rampant gift giving. If there are indications in 2015 that this is starting to change with consumers waiting for the last minute for drastic price cuts and the rise of gift cards, that too is based on a story—that there are times when people can get the best deals.

The thing about stories is that when they are told and believed and shared and considered to be true, that's when they gain power. Of course, if we're going to be scrupulously ethical, stories would always be developed from empirical evidence. But, as we all know, that's not necessary, nor is it consistent with human development.

Many of the earliest stories—what we now call myths—were designed to explain how the world works. Today, we think it's quaint or amusing or downright ridiculous that there was a time that people believed the sun was drawn across the sky by a chariot. But they did. Stories exist within the context of our experience. They make sense of the inexplicable but within the context of a culture. One only needs to look at the various cosmologies of ancient cultures to see how stories of how the world works reflect the real world inhabited by the people who told them. As science developed and a new understanding of the world evolved, the old stories were, for want of a better word, put away. They became artifacts of a vanished culture. As demonstrable facts were acquired, the story had to change to accommodate those facts.

Stories are, of course, very powerful. One need only look at the religions of the world to see how powerful stories are. People go to war and die for them. They attack people whose stories are at odds with theirs. The fact that there isn't a scrap of proof for any of them doesn't matter. Entire cultures, structures, and economies are built on the strength of these stories, so the investment in maintaining and promoting the story is critical. Not only that, but training new people in the stories and fostering their belief so they will support the cultures, structures, and economies is critical for their continuance.

It is not my intention to pick a fight with any religion or to challenge anyone's faith. My personal beliefs (and anyone's, to be frank) are irrelevant to this conversation. The point, though, is to demonstrate the power of story in creating a reality that shapes how people act and relate to others, and how it can be used to unite or divide, create or destroy value of any kind. Indeed, story is far more compelling than fact in many cases. If it weren't, the business of advertising would collapse in no time.

Before I talk about the role of story in play and its component parts, let's just take a quick look at one of the other, completely secular, story mills of the modern world: the stock market. Now, you might be aghast that I would suggest something so important and monolithic might balance on something as ephemeral as a narrative, but that's exactly what I'm saying. If you follow financial news, you've undoubtedly heard that such-and-such stock was down today on rumors of one thing or another. Or up. That story motivates behavior (buy or sell) and has a tangible impact on people's portfolios. But it really comes down to speculating on a story. Yes, that speculation may be based on years of experience and market knowledge, but you really don't know what's going to happen.

Ironically, at least with relation to stocks, if you really *do* know what's going to happen before the world knows and you tell your buddy, who buys or sells based on knowing the real story, then you've committed a crime. Despite the fact that they're taking an action based on a story, the whole structure of the Wall Street game is that you're allowed to have the story and act on your interpretation of it, but everyone has to get the facts at the same time, more or less. In committing the crime of insider trading, they've broken that rule and thus have an unfair advantage.

So if you're with me thus far, you can see that civilizations, fortunes, relationships, and careers all rise and fall on stories. And you also realize, I hope, that belief in a story is often more powerful than demonstrable facts that potentially disprove the story. This is neither good nor bad; it's simply a part of human experience. Moreover, you can use stories to create great good or great evil. If you doubt me, take a world literature course, or crack open a few Shakespeare plays. How many of the actions in Shakespeare are the direct result of stories? Pretty much all the great tragedies, the entire plot of *Much Ado About Nothing,* and the great triumph of *Henry V.* In this last instance, while the actual record of the battle of Agincourt doesn't include a rousing speech by the king before the fight, the belief that God was on the side of the English certainly drove the conflict, and the English gave God the credit.

You could go on and on with this, but I doubt you'll find many works of literature—from *Hannibal* to *The Hobbit* to *Harry Potter*—where belief driven by story hasn't been a prime motivating factor. In his 1976 study, "The Uses of Enchantment," psychologist Bruno Bettleheim gave a Freudian perspective on story, specifically, classic fairy tales, and suggested the vicarious experiences provided by reading these tales helped children grapple with conflict and the fairly sophisticated emotional experiences—death, abandonment, challenge, and more—in the abstract so as to be better prepared when they encounter those experiences in their lives.

Story is how we codify and contextualize what happens in the world and in our lives. It's important to realize that it is never what actually happens but how we interpret events and memorialize them (for want of a better word) in story that dictate action and/or belief. Ask yourself how often you have seen two vastly different interpretations of the same set of facts, and you'll soon become a believer in the power of story.

Story in Play

That said, it's axiomatic that all of us are storytellers, and understanding the uses of story in children's play can be helpful as we develop and tell our personal stories or our business stories, and it can help us use story effectively as adults.

Children tell stories to make sense of the world—to figure out where they fit in the context of a family, school, or culture. They tell stories as part of developing their personalities, as a form of competition or an essential defense. They create stories to have imaginary experiences that, even though they know them to be untrue, still create a real experience, which would otherwise be beyond their years and physical development and, quite often, impossible for humans. (This is the basic premise of Bruno Bettleheim's work mentioned earlier.) In the creation of their lives, children's stories become the ultimate user-generated content, to use a contemporary phrase.

When it comes to toys, action figures and dolls offer two kinds of toys that most children engage in. Although which toy a child plays with is often a function of gender and the play may appear different, reflecting inherent gender differences, the stories serve exactly the same developmental purposes.

These toys, to be completely literal, are nothing more than inert lumps of plastic; they couldn't be more lifeless. It's the child's imagination that gives the toys any kind of life or power. Each child's imagination is unique, and thus, though there have been billions of Barbie dolls sold, each one is similarly unique because of the power invested in it by the child playing with it. In this way, toys are totems in the Freudian sense. The child projects his or her reality onto the toy to give it life.

Think of it this way: When a child is 6 or 7, his or her life is completely dominated by the parents or caregivers. It's an endless stream of "Eat your lunch," "Get in the car," "Hurry up," and so forth. But it is also at just this time that the child is beginning to develop a sense of him- or herself as a separate individual. The fantasy of having superpowers to be free from all of this control is quite liberating—while at the same time being safe because in actuality the child is still quite dependent at that age. Superpowers allow children, at least in the imagination, to overcome the inescapable limitations of being a kid. In this imaginative exercise, the feeling of confidence is real, regardless of how the child got there, and it can be stored away for future use.

Story in play also helps children make sense of what they're experiencing, to process emotions and information, and always reflects the individual's perceived reality. Many years ago, I was observing a little girl who was playing with her Barbie dolls in the play scenario that she had created: Three blonde dolls were teasing the one brunette doll—ostracizing her, really. The brunette doll, however, stood her ground in the play scenario. As you might guess, this reflected a situation she was having as a new kid in her preschool who was trying to make friends and fit in. Play, in this instance, provided a literal rehearsal for her life. Whether she ultimately solved this issue is not necessarily relevant. The point is the story and the play around that story allowed her to have an experience of processing her emotions and the situation, and figuring out various ways of dealing with the situation. There was no risk, as she controlled all the variables at that time and could try on various different responses and outcomes.

Story is also a key component of social interaction among children. When a kid in a playgroup, for example, gets everyone to play Batman, each child becomes invested in the story. They create a reality around the story that, though it exists only in their imaginations, forms the basis for interaction and play. More importantly, they are all working from the same inherent story of the Batman character and his world because they have internalized their versions of the story as part of their individual experience of the story from other sources. And that's when something amazing happens: As the story becomes more and more real to the players, they begin telling the story themselves, adding their embellishments and personal information. The story no longer belongs to one child; it belongs to the group. At the same time, it's important to remember that, though there is a group narrative, how the different elements of that narrative are perceived is going to vary.

Not surprisingly, this can lead to conflict. Arguments can erupt among children when their personal version of the story varies from what the group is doing. For example:

"Batman can't do that!"

"Yes, he can."

"No, he can't."

Although this may sound like childish bickering—and it is, actually—the larger purpose is to be able to align story elements so the process can move forward. This type of argument usually leads to negotiation and resolution of one sort or another, and either the play continues with some variation or it falls apart. Adults viewing this kind of dispute tend to become uncomfortable and want to swoop in and resolve it. Of course, this is probably the worst thing an adult can do. Provided that the argument doesn't turn violent or devolve into name-calling or some such, this is a time when kids learn to resolve issues among themselves.

One of the greatest disservices one can do to children is not to allow them to resolve their playground issues themselves. And yet, we see this all the time. Adults who believe that conflict is somehow damaging to children fail to understand that what's learned on the playground in a relatively safe environment sets the stage for future interactions. A child conditioned to expect outside intervention for conflict resolution is ill equipped for the adult world.

Story in play, finally, sows the seeds of self-perception and self-knowledge. The stories children tell about themselves and that are told about them are the essential building blocks of identity. Humans are changeable, but stories tend to stick around and acquire a level of permanence which, though not necessarily accurate, is responded to as if it were immutable.

Try this little exercise: Think about the last argument you had with a friend, spouse, or co-worker. What prompted it? I'm guessing it had something to do with a story you created about an action that person took. Did your spouse forget to do something that prompted you to say, "You always do X!"?

Now, think about it: If your partner *always* does something, should you be surprised and angry when he or she does it? So my question for you is: What is the story that you are telling about your relationship?

Similarly, in the workplace people get reputations because others tell stories about them. Those stories become enshrined as myths, and those myths get believed and become a reality unto themselves.

If you have siblings, you probably have a family hierarchy where each one is known as "the _____ one." (Feel free to fill in the blank as it relates to your unique situation.)

These stories have become your reality from repeated telling, though that doesn't necessarily make them true. Yet, you most likely respond to every person and every situation through your response to those stories.

We all can agree about the details of the Superman story—flying, strength, avoiding Kryptonite, and so forth—because someone else made up the story, and willingly suspending disbelief is part of the fun of engaging in his adventures. It's more difficult to see what might not be true in our own stories when we've made them up. If we are highly responsible, detail-oriented people, we don't think that remembering to pick up the dry cleaning is a superhuman feat. But that's just our own story. It might actually be very difficult for someone else. It may not be their play style, to continue what was described earlier.

Now, imagine how you might rewrite the story so it takes into account the person who simply can't remember to pick up the dry cleaning. You can still be the hero, but perhaps in this revision you're rescuing the person rather than destroying them with a death ray. You can make it up any way you choose, but the stories are going to have different outcomes, and as with the play scenario described previously, that's going to set the stage for the next chapter in the story.

The points of this exercise are to begin to understand the ways in which we make up our lives and to realize our own power as the story-teller, or the person behind the play. What you have imagined affects your behavior and interactions. And that most of the time, what we consider "reality" is something we made up.

So, you might say that we are always playing in the purest sense of the word. Reality, and anything we do, begins in the imagination, and the stories we create and tell, as we'll see, are one of the most important parts of play—and the one we don't leave behind as we go from childhood to adulthood.

The Structuring of Stories

When you come right down to it, all business is telling stories. And story impacts all aspects of businesses for companies and for individuals. Isolating the ways in which story can be crafted and used is an essential tool that can make the difference between success and failure.

Let's just look at one critical area to start: company valuations. Company valuations are based on actual past performance. But what about the future? How does a CEO mitigate a stock slide after a damaging quarter? Through story. He or she can't know wholly what the future looks like and probably has incomplete information about it, but a well-crafted story that is both believable and targeted to the correct ears can save the day. Investors don't want to hear that a CEO has lost his or her way and has no idea how the company is going to pull out of a current downturn. Even if that's partially true, that's going to cause a panic in the investment community. And so a story is crafted that people want to hear that allays fears, offers hope for the future, and is plausible. If you doubt this, go read the press releases from companies that have had bad quarters and ask yourself how many of these things are really knowable. As with Shakespeare's *Henry V,* mentioned earlier, the story was what inspired the belief to fight; it certainly wasn't the facts. Taking just the facts—outnumbered, faced with illness, up to their knees in mud, and so on—no rational person would have stuck around, regardless of the fact that Henry prevailed. And that's one of the key powers of story: It overrides the rational.

In fact, all of reality is telling stories. The stories we tell today become our reality. The more we tell them, the more real they become, and people begin to act *as if* the stories are real. And sooner or later those stories are real.

This is where engaging in the storytelling nature of play is so essential to success in business. How you tell your stories, to whom you tell them, and the nature of the story are all elements that need to be addressed—along with the fact that stories change over time.

It's probably an exaggeration, but for many professions, and certainly in marketing and product development, as we'll discuss shortly, storytelling is probably a significant portion of your job. The current buzzword is "narrative," but that's just a more formal way of saying "story." Really.

So, let's look at what makes a good story. Children's book author Bill Doyle, who has written several successful series of chapter books, describes stories with a hand acronym: COWS, which stands for:

Conflict

Omit Yourself

What Do They Want?

Stakes

Conflict

This is essential to any story, or else why would you even bother reading? Conflict is what engages people and involves them on a personal level. Will Dorothy beat the Wicked Witch? Can Harry Potter overcome Voldemort? As Doyle says, "a gently flowing stream may be lovely to look at, but will it hold your interest for hundreds of pages or three hours?" And, of course, the answer is no.

We tend to think of conflict as a negative, but is it? Conflict can be full of anger and aggression, but more often than not it's more benign. In everyday life, it is simply what leads up to the point of choice. It is seldom as dramatic as in fiction, but it is nonetheless real. It can be as seemingly rational as a consumer choosing which television to buy from the plethora of brands available or what to select from a menu.

For marketers in particular, identifying the conflict is essential if you're going to tell a compelling story. It goes beyond simply identifying who your competitors are; it involves delving into your competitors story as deeply as your own. Only then can you craft a story that creates conflict in a consumer's mind. Marketing expert Jennifer Deare, who has specialized in developing successful competitive programs for a variety of consumer products companies, notes that in telling a story, a marketer has to analyze the competition and the market situation in the context of the product they are trying to promote. The goal is to identify potential weaknesses that can be leveraged in promotion, essentially creating conflict for the consumer by sowing doubt. "Of course, you can't just come out and say, 'X brand is evil' in the way you can in a story," she says. Instead, you have to analyze your competitors' stories and find a way of telling your own that opens the door to another way of thinking about a product or service. This leads logically to the next element Doyle identifies as inherent to a good story.

Omit Yourself

In terms of fiction, this means that if you, as the author, are a character in the story, the observational position tends to undermine the effectiveness of a story unless that character takes an active role in the events. The essential lesson of this is to try to eliminate anything that tends to slow down narrative.

The translation to business applications is slightly subtler than the issue of conflict, but it is nonetheless critical, particularly in marketing, where companies sometimes get so caught up in their own brand identity and imagery that they lose sight of what their customers' experiences are.

A major toy brand was experiencing lackluster sales and struggling in a changing marketplace. The internal conversations were about what the brand meant, and weeks and months were invested in a discussion about the brand that was never resolved. Product suffered in the meantime because the story they were telling had no relevance to the consumer. Only with a change of management and a renewed attention to the customer experience did the brand begin to rebound. Essentially, they had dug themselves an intellectual hole that allowed them to fill countless decks, have seemingly endless meetings, and yet not move forward.

I don't want to pick on one brand. This type of thinking is very common. And it happens, in our experience, because people are afraid to take a stand. It's far easier to talk about things in the abstract and make everyone feel good than it is to take an action that might very well fail. This is the avoidance of conflict and the admission of not knowing, which makes a pretty lame story, when you come right down to it.

So, how do you as a businessperson omit yourself? It may at first seem counterintuitive, and, in fact, you can't really omit yourself, or your product or company, from a conversation, which for purposes of this discussion we'll refer to as a character. In this case, you have to give the character something to do.

On a practical level, one of the things we have insisted upon is the limitation of internal conversations about such things as "Brand DNA." What does that mean, anyway? When I have to sit through endless presentations about minutiae that don't relate to getting the job done or selling a product, my eyes tend to glaze over. This is talking to oneself, and many people do it because it's safe. Yes, I know that in a presentation, it's important for the client to know you understand who they are. But, really, take a hint from the best stories: Show me; don't tell me. Or, better yet, cut to the chase. The problem, of course, is that if you're not regurgitating or navel gazing (sorry to all you "strategic marketers" if you take umbrage at that statement. That's how so much of this stuff is only valid when it gets you closer to action.), you're going to be forced into making a commitment, and that's scary because it goes back to the topic we discussed earlier of not knowing precisely what the results are going to be.

Stories—and especially stories in play—are about action. When you watch kids engaged in role play, which is simply the process of pretending to be characters, whether of one's own devising or based on entertainment, you quickly see that there is very little time invested in the setup because they all know the backstory, as it were. For businesspeople—and marketers in particular—the less time you need to spend in setup, the more time you can spend playing.

In practical terms, we generally advise no more than three to five slides or pages in a proposal to set the stage in a meeting, and then only when there are people who don't know the story.

This is truly omitting oneself and clearing the path to get right into the play. When we suggest this to clients, we sometimes get pushback about people who might not be prepared for a meeting or need more information. That should happen before the meeting begins. Think of it this way: When a child joins a group of kids playing, there's very little time invested in bringing the new kid up to speed on the backstory. He or she either jumps in and makes the most of it, or removes him- or herself from the game. If the kid wants to play with these others again, you can bet he or she will watch the show, read the book, and be prepared to engage.

This shows up in creative meetings all the time. When we run brainstorming sessions for clients, everyone invited receives the briefing materials prior to the session. Those who've taken the time to prepare generally perform much better and offer more in the creative meeting. Those who do not find themselves running to catch up, don't participate fully, and aren't ready to play—often in front of their boss and perhaps their boss's boss.

The bottom line is that it's your job to be fully invested in all of the goals and stories that impact your job function. Just like kids at play, no one is going to do it for you.

What Do They Want?

This is the primary driver of every story—and much play. In business and/or marketing terms, it's often referred to as the objective. Getting what you want, or falling short, is the prime determinant of a story and certainly whether or not it's interesting. If we don't care if Hamlet avenges his father's death, Harry Potter defeats Voldemort, or Neely O'Hara makes a comeback (to run the gamut from the sublime to the ridiculous), the story falls flat.

In play, kids are intently objective-focused. If you've ever tried to wrangle a toddler determined to grab something off a table, you've experienced this firsthand. You move the kid away. He or she comes back. You try again. He or she tries again. You move the object to a higher place, and you see a pair of little eyes follow your actions.

Skateboarding is another great example. Kids will practice a trick for hours, knowing that they may or may not hit it.

The point of both of these examples is that clear objectives are essential for any aspect of business. When we review marketing programs, it's also one of the largest things that's lacking. It comes down to a deceptively simple statement of what you want to accomplish, but there's another factor that has to be included: It has to be measurable.

When the kid hits the skateboard trick, the objective is achieved. It's absolutely unambiguous. When the toddler does or does not snatch the figurine from the coffee table, the result is clear.

Muddy objectives—those that are not specific and measurable— tend to lead to muddy processes and unclear results. Yet, we constantly find that unclear objectives are far more the norm. In probing this issue over the years, largely with marketers, it becomes clear that there is often an investment in, for want of a better word, squishy objectives. They minimize accountability, and provide "cover" and wiggle room. This is, perhaps, an understandable position. We once asked a middle manager at a major company what his career strategy was, and he replied, "Keep my head down and don't get blamed." It worked for a while. He survived the first three rounds of cuts, but ultimately he lost his job and had a difficult time finding another one.

And you wonder why people wish they could be kids again. Can you imagine a kid spending an entire afternoon trying to master a skateboard trick without actually doing it? Where's the fun or investment in that? Now, in the instance of the middle manager, you might easily say his objective was not to lose his job. Fine. But who wants someone on their team like that?

The point of clear objectives in crafting your story is not wholly whether or not you achieve them. They are a guide that allows you to determine progress and change course as you go. In a story, it's those twists and turns that add excitement. Just think of all the times Jason Bourne and Indiana Jones have to change course. They don't decide to sit it out or get killed when things don't go according to plan. They have to figure out a new way to get around things. This is the adventure that kids play. Particularly in action figure or role-play, the child always imagines him- or herself as the one who can overcome the obstacle. Now, there are very few business or marketing challenges that are literally analogous to being crushed by a runaway boulder. But, actually, think about that. Declining sales lead to decreased revenues and lead to depressed stock prices. And your business, or career, is crushed.

Business, like the imagination, thrives on being fluid and responsive. Market conditions are constantly changing. Competition is cropping up out of nowhere. Even when people set clear and measurable objectives, one of the consistent problems we see is that reviewing them doesn't become part of the daily process. A client sets an objective, develops a plan, and goes for it. Only at the end of the process do they stop to see whether or not they've achieved it. As any kid trying to hit a skateboard trick knows, there are hundreds of chances to refine what you're doing and get you closer to achieving your objectives.

Defining "What do they want?" or objectives is generally the first step in telling a story. After all, what we're talking about here is what leads up to telling the story—starting the adventure.

Stakes

A key element of any story is the stakes. That is, what's at risk if the objective is not achieved? If Dorothy doesn't get the broomstick of the Witch of the West, she can't get home, for example. They are what drive a story and add tension to it. They provide resonance and context for objectives. In a business context, the stakes are often rather obvious: gained market share, increased sales, and so forth. In a story, the stakes work in conjunction with what each character wants to guide action.

In business, identifying and analyzing the stakes should become central to guiding action. Like the objectives, stakes can focus and inspire action. Especially in marketing programs, you always have to consider the stakes and whether or not your efforts are going to help you achieve your objectives.

When I was working on a dog food account years ago, there were many attractive opportunities, but the central question always came down to "Does it sell dog food?" If we didn't sell dog food, we lost. More importantly, if we couldn't show how it was going to sell dog food—and sell enough to offset the cost of the program by a significant margin—we didn't do it.

Similarly, we see all kinds of promotions that gratify the egos of executives or marketing managers, cost a great deal of money, and don't move the needle one bit when it comes to sales. Everyone gets to congratulate themselves on an event that may have come off well, but if it doesn't achieve measurable results, it may have been a waste of time and money.

The point of this is exercise is to encourage you to be ruthless in defining and telling your story. Children engaged in story-based play tend to be very focused and driven. There are many reasons we lose this in business: politics, expediency, an unwillingness to create conflict, and so on. However, what story worth anything has ever existed without conflict?

Knowing Your Audience

There is an old show-biz adage: Give 'em what they want. This couldn't be more relevant to business. Although your story may strive to create a need in a consumer's mind where none existed previously, you must also speak to that consumer's mindset and understanding. We'll talk more about this when we talk about research a little bit later on.

For the moment, though, consider how children become engaged in something during play. Something in a story grabs their attention, and they are sucked in. To fully appreciate this, however, you need to understand how children perceive things. A story that is too complicated or not relevant will be ignored. Children in play feel no compunction to address or even acknowledge something that isn't directly relevant to them.

Guess what? Neither do adults. The difference is that children don't have the developed social structure that expects them to at least make an effort.

So, you have to tell your story in a way that, like any toy, inspires your audience to tell the story themselves—for, as with kids, it's the stories that they make up that have the most power. Just as a kid brings Barbie or Teenage Mutant Ninja Turtles to life by retelling and adapting the basic story to their own experience, so too much of your job as a marketer is to get people to tell your story in their own way and in their own lives, which leads us to...

Brands as Stories

For businesses, the *story* is the *brand*. And brands have never been more important than they are today. In a crowded, competitive, and fragmented market, telling the story is not enough. You have to use the story to invite customers to play along—to make them *want* to play along and make the story their own.

In fact, every brand, like every superhero, has its own established story—a kind of mythos, really—and when that story is deeply understood both at the business and the consumer levels, then it's possible to play—to elaborate on that story.

That's the power of story in the process of branding. It's not just the one-way telling of the story that gives a story life and truth; it's the moment at which the consumer starts telling the story for you. It is, in the purest sense, the evangelizing of consumerism.

Marketers can impose all the stories they want on the public, but until the point when the consumer takes over the storytelling role, there is no brand. We define a brand as an ingrained belief in and expectation of a specific experience developed *over time.* It is only when a story passes into myth that a brand can be considered established.

As any marketer knows, brand loyalty is a very powerful thing. And it's not empirical data, but experience augmented by belief that creates it. Does Tide really get my clothes cleaner than another brand? I have no idea, and neither have you. Or at least, I doubt you've ever done the kind of scientific analysis that would give you that definitive answer. You see clean clothes after doing the laundry, and you believe that Tide did that. You might even have tried another brand and thought the clothes were not as clean. Was that true, or was that a reflection of your disappointment that they were out of Tide at the supermarket? You'll probably never know. And there is the essence of advertising and marketing since the dawn of the industry. An individual's belief and natural inclination to create stories around everything in his or her life are the greatest selling tools there are.

Kids from the 1960s probably remember a brand of sneakers named PF Flyers. A second-place brand to then-leader Keds, PF Flyers emerged from relative obscurity with a single advertising claim: They make you run faster and jump higher. This message repeated over and over on Saturday morning television inspired an entire generation of kids to demand PF Flyers with the dream that they would go from being the last kid picked for a team to a star athlete just by tightening their laces.

The idea of an object conferring superhuman power is a staple of literature—and a favorite fantasy. Don Quixote waylaid a barber and tried to take his shaving basin, believing it was the golden helmet of Mambrino that would make him invincible. Harry Potter had the cloak of invisibility. Tolkein and Wagner were partial to rings. Dumbo had his feather, to dip into anthropomorphism for a moment. Finding a way to overcome our real or perceived vulnerabilities is a driving human characteristic, and the idea of some object imbued with totemic power is an integral part of the wish fulfillment that is at the heart of stories and brands.

The real world of 1960s marketing and the world of mythical creatures splashing about in the Rhine share the power of story in bringing both to life. Many kids were disappointed that they still did not excel on the playing field, and today marketing to children in that way is forbidden.

It is still a staple of marketing and advertising. The energy drink Red Bull marketed itself under the claim that it "gives you wings." Most reasonable adults would acknowledge that this was an abstraction and grant the brand poetic license. Not Benjamin Careathers, however. In

2013, he sued the brand, saying that, having consumed it over time, he did not acquire wings or even increased, wingless, performance. The suit was settled out of court and cost the company about $13 million in potential refunds. What's important about this—over and above the fact that Red Bull has not been proven to deliver anything more than a generous serving of caffeine—is that it was never the actual product that was being challenged: It was the story.

It is the belief in a story that gives it its power to control action. In his 1889 short story "Gooseberries," Anton Chekhov makes the point in a typically trenchant fashion. A wealthy nobleman has succeeded in growing gooseberries, and they are served to a guest with great ceremony. The nobleman eats them with relish, asserting their superiority in every respect. His guest, the narrator, however, finds them "hard and sour." He quotes Pushkin, saying, "The illusion which exalts us is better than ten thousand truths." This throws the narrator into despair, as he cannot rationalize the happiness that belief in the illusion offers against "the silent protest of statistics." Ultimately—this being Chekhov, after all—he comes to believe that happiness based on beliefs is a type of "general hypnosis." And indeed it is.

Call us wizards, spellbinders, or hypnotists, that is the role of marketers. Chekhov's narrator is forced ultimately to admit that the illusions do no harm and may, in fact, create a foundation for greater happiness.

It should be clear by now that a powerfully crafted, well-told story embraced by consumers will always trump literal truth. Sub-Zero refrigerators cost thousands of dollars, are often plagued with problems, and are difficult to maintain. A Kenmore refrigerator costing a fraction as much will keep milk just as cold, but it has no story that enhances its value by a factor of eight or more. Yet Sub-Zero is booming and families are stretching their budgets to have that $7,500 fridge in the kitchen. Why? Because they are involved in the story. They now tell the Sub-Zero story to themselves and to everyone in their sphere of influence.

These stories have very real results. Pick a successful brand and take apart its story. Delve into the characters and largely the character of the consumer. Penetrate his or her beliefs and how to speak to them. Then look at how you tell your own. It all starts with the very same spark of imagination a child discovers when he or she says, "Let's pretend...."

Social Media: A New Playground

In this marketplace where commodities reign and the DVR allows commercials to be zapped, marketers have to become wizards and develop new tactics. In other words, they have to learn to cast spells, and they have to use newer, rougher magic to bypass a consumer increasingly tuned out from traditional advertising.

Enter social media. From a storytelling standpoint, this is unprecedented because it allows the individual voice to be magnified exponentially. It's also fraught with dangers because it takes the control of the storytelling out of your hands, to some extent. This inevitably changes how your stories are being told, and it significantly changes your role as the storyteller.

The world of social media is a crazy sandbox, which at times seems tailor-made to drive marketers and companies crazy.

As online and social media continues to develop and evolve, we see dynamic evolution of platforms and interaction that boggle the mind. Things are changing every six months, give or take, and it forces a level of fluidity on companies that doesn't fit easily in many business structures.

Yet it's critically important. For the kid who is responding to changing conditions, new ideas, or different input, shifting gears is often quick and without a lot of questioning. Now, I'm not suggesting that a company abandon all structure, but the world of social media is rough and tumble, and if you don't keep up, you're out of the game.

The thing about social media in the context of storytelling is that it's a two-way action. The story you're telling is not always the one that's being responded to, but you have to be ready for everything that's thrown at you, from customer outrage to change.org petitions to—yes, it happens—stalking.

Most importantly, the old methods aren't working, and it's a world full of new rules and new language. Most importantly, it's a world that's dominated by young people. They're native to a lot of these technologies and platforms, adopt them early, and master them quickly. Their insights and ideas are invaluable, and they have an inherent understanding of how storytelling is changing. Whether Instagram, Snapchat, Facebook, Twitter, or other platforms, social media is changing the rules of engagement and giving formerly relatively passive, consumers a more active role in the overall storytelling.

It's imperative to know how to manage this. Take the company that wants to approve six months of tweets at one time. That's hardly realistic given the nature of Twitter, but fully understandable in the realm of corporate responsibility and legal protection, and avoiding situations like the Red Bull lawsuit mentioned earlier. The rules have changed, though, and structures must change to reflect that.

In this new world, storytelling and play really can really shine. As mentioned, when you have your audience so enrolled in your story that they're telling it form their perspective to people who listen to them, that's a success. Take a look at all the LEGO videos on YouTube, for example. These are things that company would not, and potentially could not, do. Fans posting their work—literally playing with the brand—help keep it top of mind and build a community around it.

In 2103, a small craft toy called the Rainbow Loom created a sensation among kids. It was never advertised on television at the outset, and it was about as low-tech as you could imagine. It was simply rubber bands, a pegboard, and a crochet hook. With these, kids could make all kinds of elastic bracelets and other items. These were then shared and given to adoring parents and grandparents, who dutifully wore them to work. Yet it was storytelling that fueled the craze and kept it going for more than a year. Despite the low-tech nature of the toy, it was technology that drove the craze, specifically YouTube videos created by its legions of fans. More than 150,000 videos were created and shared, many of them how-tos, which effectively established a community around this product. By the end of 2014, the craze had passed and the market moved on, but this is a tribute to the power of an engaged consumer telling his or her own story.

Chances are if you never heard of the Rainbow Loom and didn't watch any of the videos, you're like the child who is able to filter out that which has no direct relevance to his or her life. It's that simple. Now, what social media has created is a community that leverages the most high-tech form of communications for a decidedly low-tech product. This puts huge demands on social media marketers to be more fluid than ever before and not rely on the tactics of what is often considered "traditional" media.

There are also dangers and pitfalls because, as many people know, the Internet can get ugly. This is an environment where opinion dominates fact. Just look at the stories told about vaccinations: A study indicates that vaccinations may cause autism. It's picked up by a celebrity who uses social and traditional media to spout this, convincing parents not to vaccinate their children. Even when the study is proven to be flawed, the story and the opinion persist. In 2015, we have outbreaks of measles, whooping cough, and potentially, polio.

There is also a great deal of misinterpretation of things like "Likes" on Facebook, or up votes, or some such. Although these are bruited about by marketers as indications of the popularity of a brand, they do not signify anything more than a passing engagement. Because it's generally impossible to determine what motivated someone to click on something, the numbers ultimately are essentially meaningless. That doesn't mean that people aren't spinning them like crazy. What's required, though, are somewhat more sophisticated numbers that actually measure engagement over time, rather than a fast-twitch mouse click. Our goal here is not to talk about data mining but to encourage you to find out how successfully your story is being told. Fortunately, there are many metrics available that savvy companies are employing to go beyond the superficial numbers.

The other major change that social media has brought to storytelling is that it is more a dialogue than ever before. True, the dialogue can sometimes be frustrating and chock-full of idiocy. Just read the comments of most political blogs and you'll see a combination of ego, ignorance, and illiteracy that is at times staggering. Though most of this is discounted, reviewing these over a period of months from all political positions indicates that, regardless of political positioning, it's so much shouting in an echo chamber, but it still indicates how anyone with a keyboard and an opinion can potentially derail your storytelling.

For marketers, however, it's important to be vigilant about how your story is being told. Responding to complaints within 24 hours, answering accusations, and taking what control of the story you can is essential—particularly so given that broader, more mainstream media will pick up on things like petitions at change.org, and your story can soon take on a life of its own. How you manage that is critical, particularly because, especially in the world of social media, outrage is often the default emotion. I'll leave it to someone else to break down the sociology of this in today's world, but we suspect it has to do with a phenomenon we call attention deficit disorder—as in "I'm not getting enough attention." I mean this glibly and in no way want to imply that the medical condition of ADD is not serious, but in a culture when anyone with a keyboard potentially has a national or even international audience, keepers of stories can't afford to take their eyes off how their story is being appropriated and retold in the market.

In 2012, toymaker Hasbro was the subject of an online petition that garnered more than 40,000 signatures from a little girl who felt the pink and purple Easy Bake Oven negatively stereotyped gender and alienated her younger brother, who wanted to play with it as well. The colors, however, indicated that it was just for girls. Out of the nearly 320 million people in the United States at the time, 40,000 are a barely measurable percent (0.0125). Still, as we've been saying, stories don't care about statistics. The story was picked up by news organizations across the country, and Hasbro was pilloried for being insensitive to children. Hasbro's marketing team even got famous male chefs to say that they had wanted Easy Bake Ovens as kids but their parents hadn't given them to them because it was a toy for girls. Ultimately, the company invited the little girl and her family to Pawtucket, where they gave her a sneak peek at the black and silver Easy Bake slated for introduction later that year.

Here's how the story got played, and—spoiler alert—it had nothing to do with reality. The little girl was presented as having an impact on a great big company, mustering the force of consumer outrage at the great big company's insensitivity, and educating them about being more aware that today's boys aren't crippled by traditional gender roles. Hasbro was seen as taking this issue seriously and acknowledging the little girl, and was, perhaps, a little humbled in the process. As it got played in the media, it was a happy ending, and the story was over.

The little girl was seen as the hero of the story, Hasbro emerged as newly enlightened, and the comparatively sleepy Easy Bake Oven had a refreshed and positive image.

Why did this work so effectively? Well, first it played into several popular stories in our culture: the David vs. Goliath type of myth; big companies are insensitive to little people and out of touch with the contemporary world; "a child shall lead them." Blah blah blah. The media picks up on these stories because they know they're popular, and will trigger responses, and get people talking and keep them watching their advertisers. It's classic storytelling with all of the elements of a good story we discussed earlier.

Here, however, is the reality, and the outcome described above is a tribute to the skill of Hasbro's storytelling, and a bit of serendipity. The Easy Bake Oven was introduced in 1963, and over the years the many redesigns have had more to do with kitchen décor than gender. Given the boom in black and stainless appliances, the Hasbro designers planned to introduce a version that would be more like the kitchens kids saw around them (just as the teal version in 1963 reflected a very popular kitchen color at the time). The product had been in the works for more than a year, and we had seen a prototype well before the crusading tween ever started her petition.

But here's where the brilliance comes in: If one goes back and reads the statements that Hasbro made on this issue, the company never publicly addressed the gender issue, other than to note they had used images of boys on packages. When the little girl saw the black and silver oven, she took over the storytelling. It was her bias that pink was for girls and black for boys that took over the story. (How that story became entrenched in our culture and accepted as true could be the subject of another study altogether.) It was her feeling that she'd been acknowledged that colored (pun intended) everything that she saw. Like the nobleman with the Gooseberries, she made what she experienced fit the storyline that she had in her mind—as did the media. Having been cast as the hero with clear conflict, the stakes were that she remain as such, so she ensured that everything could be manipulated to provide the perception that she got what she wanted. What mattered was the happy ending, and everyone got what they wanted.

For Hasbro, it cost them virtually nothing, and I by no means want to imply that there was anything cynical or manipulative in what they did. They simply understood the stories that were being told and recognized that their involvement—and not hiding from it—would give them a role in the story that was going to be told whether or not they got involved. Just to look at one element of the story—that the company was out of touch with contemporary gender roles—is really a no-win if they engage in that story. So, instead, they brought the girl who had accused them to their offices, showed her something new, and let the girl tell the story. Yes, it's a classic PR move, I suppose, but at the same time the company never took a public position. In this case, for the "hero" to discover for herself that she has gotten what she wanted, however that came about, is much more powerful in a storytelling vein.

As difficult as these situations can be for companies, you really have to keep them in perspective. At one time or another, you or your company may get caught up in a story that is not of your making. How you respond determines the difference between a success and a failure, and as we keep saying, the story can often be more powerful than the truth. Any marketer knows it is the rare consumer products company that is completely out of touch with its consumers. They spend hundreds of thousands, if not millions, of dollars to learn about their consumers. It would be foolish not to. Hasbro, in particular, has been highly successful at leveraging consumer insights into successful products. Those facts, however, can't always compete with a popular story. Knowing how to manage that story is where the real play comes in. Being willing to work with the parameters of a story and its own, for want of a better word, integrity is essential and requires imagination. Companies get bogged down when they try to take a hard corporate line. Remember: You can't battle an entrenched story with facts. Perhaps in court, but not in the marketplace.

The ultimate reality, however, is that whatever the stories, when you're selling a product, the market always decides. One year after Easy Bake–gate (sorry, couldn't resist), the story was virtually forgotten (for now). Oh, and the pink and purple Easy Bake Oven outsold the black and silver one by a hefty margin.

We overlook or devalue the power of story at our peril. Stories are powerful and personal. They are how we understand the world and build our identities. We start them as children, but we tell them throughout our lives. They can drive us, or drive us crazy, and they shape our reality. You are, in fact, your own Scheherazade, whose stories not only enchanted a king but kept her alive as well.

Play vs. Recreation

At this point, it's time to make an important distinction: the difference between play and recreation.

Both are hugely important and offer lots of benefits in terms of well-being and productivity. However, they serve very different functions, and though both can inspire creativity in a business setting, they do it in different ways.

The distinction, as we're defining it here, is that play is an immersive, conscious process that opens us up to new ways of thinking and new solutions, whereas recreation is a distraction—a break, if you will, from playing.

The confusion arises partly out of semantics. As we said at the outset, the word "play" is taken to connote a lack of seriousness that, especially for adults, is synonymous with recreation. Hopefully, though, by this point you've begun to see play in a different light: as an inherent human characteristic that needs to be fostered and directed in order to enhance creativity at all levels of work and life. Play, as we're talking about it, is highly focused, conscious, and intention-driven.

If you watch a child who is immersed in play, you see the intention with which he or she attacks the situation, whether it's acting out a story, practicing a sport, or being involved in any creative activity. The task at hand is all-consuming. You may have had the experience of calling a child to dinner repeatedly only to have them not respond. It is not, necessarily, that they are being intractable or resistant. It may, in fact, be because they literally don't hear you. This is part of the makeup of the brain that allows one to focus so closely on the task at hand that the other senses are diminished. If you have been calling for half an hour, the child may truly have only heard you the last time you called. This is actually a good thing; it means your child has the capacity to focus and shut out other distractions—which, unfortunately, may sometimes be that increasingly frustrated parent or caregiver.

You might be tempted to call this "attention" instead of "play." As we discuss it, attention is a component of play, but it is separate. Attention is the focus necessary to engage in the active process of play in which one is constantly weighing different actions and different potential outcomes. The goal, at least if one is trying to facilitate change, is to bring a level of consciousness to the process for any task at hand. It is about conceiving different actions and different outcomes, and giving oneself the freedom to take them. In this case, play becomes so much larger than attention.

Recreation, on the other hand, is about distraction, or at least changing focus. It's designed to give the brain a break from all the intense activity that's going on. Just by the nature of being mammals, our minds can only hold so much at any given time, and it takes time to process what we have experienced on both conscious and unconscious levels. Taking a break and changing focus allows the unconscious to work and have other ideas. If you've ever had the experience of being stuck on a problem only to have a possible solution pop into your mind as you're running, walking to your car, or cleaning the garage, you've experienced the creative power of recreation. You have literally freed up your mind to do its processing job in the background and spit out a possible solution into your consciousness, so to speak. In his insightful book *The Organized Mind: Thinking Straight in the Age of Information Overload*, Daniel J. Levitin explains the neuroscience behind all of this and our inherently messy brains that are clogged with all manner of information, with more coming in at each moment.

Much has been written about companies that install foosball tables or basketball courts, hire massage therapists, build rock-climbing walls, and so forth. It's very cool to think of having a place where you can go and "chill" on a break, or that you have an adult version of Chuck E. Cheese's at work. Companies that provide this type of recreation environment are often considered forward-thinking and are ranked highly as places to work, but aside from the great PR and the romantic notion that you can accomplish something important as you try to land a bank shot on the pool table, there is nothing to say that one form of recreation is more effective than another at helping with your brain function.

As with play, there are as many styles of recreation as there are people. The point is that human beings need the change of energy and the physical benefits that come from moving. And once again, we need look no further than children's experiences to understand how beneficial and important this is.

Recess and the shrinking time devoted to it has been a hot topic among parents and educators certainly since the early 2000s. As educators are feeling more and more stress to be productive during school hours and the growth of standardized testing looms large, recess time has been chipped away in favor of class time. But human beings, especially kids in elementary school, are not designed to sit still and be crammed with information for hours at a time. Biologically, that is unnatural for us as creatures. We can learn it, but it doesn't come naturally. So, allowing kids to run around and blow off steam is essential. The chemicals released into the body actually help kids concentrate.

Nor does recreation have to be as intently active as hanging from the monkey bars. Art therapist Addie Dix-McCabe describes how physical work with manipulative materials like clay release the same chemicals into the bloodstream and allow kids to concentrate.

My own work with theater games with junior high school kids who were deemed "difficult" showed that when given a chance to be physical and creative as a break from studies, these kids were significantly better at concentrating, enjoyed their studies more, and became more participatory in all classes than students who did not get a break or whose "acting out" was treated with drugs.

The bottom line is that we are physical creatures, and managers need to take that into account. Moreover, this type of recreation is not all that time-consuming. You don't need to open a Dave & Buster's outpost or install a bowling alley (though I'd kind of like to bowl more). A walk around the block, going out and climbing a few floors of stairs, or keeping Play-Doh at your desk can do it. You know those popular stress balls people have? They work, and as Dix-McCabe points out, the physical release is the same as if you were working with paints or clay. (You just don't have something to hang on the refrigerator when you're done.)

Two essential aspects of recreation that we have observed are that for it to be effective it has to be physical and it has to be done regularly. You need to get up from your desk and move. That's the only way you can release the chemicals that you need to enhance concentration and memory. You can't take a pill, use a patch, or pop a supplement. Movement also stimulates the part of the brain that stimulates concentration and memory. John J. Ratey has done extensive scientific work in this area, and although his research covers more intense exercise programs, our interviews indicate that people who do something different during work breaks, whether it's taking a spin class (high exertion) or window shopping (low exertion), report that they are better able to focus on tasks when they return.

This is a huge argument for not having lunch at one's desk. In fact, people who do not do something physical during the day and who spend their lunch hour looking online, whether looking at news blogs, shopping, or looking at porn (yes, they do), do not report anywhere near the level of stress reduction or ability to concentrate after that type of break.

Taking care of your own recreation, as well as fostering an environment where that's possible for others, can be highly effective at increasing productivity. And it's probably important to point out that this is separate from the company softball team or some other kind of organized activity, which may not be relevant to or involve everyone. Most importantly, these activities should be individual to each person and shouldn't be competitive. Most offices are competitive enough without adding another level of competition to non-essential work.

So, here are some tips you can use to foster that important recreational (in all senses of the word) time without turning your break room into a boardwalk arcade:

- If you're lucky enough to have a company gym, encourage employees to use it. If not, look into getting a group rate at a local club.

- Try not to schedule too many meetings that require people to work through breaks. If you have to, ensure that it's the exception rather than the rule. Think back to how rotten it was in school when gym or recess got cancelled.

- If you're a manager, model this practice. You'll benefit from it as well, and you create an environment where people feel it's okay to do what the boss is doing.

- Depending on your workplace, you may be able to have some recreational items in the office. In my office, we have NERF guns, balls, and all kinds of paraphernalia that let people blow off steam and laugh. I would hate to see that in my lawyer's office, however.

- Understand that employees of different ages have different approaches to work based on where they fit culturally as a function of their ages (always acknowledging that these characteristics won't apply across the board to every individual). This may be helpful for understanding where you fit into the cultural context and, if you're a manager, understanding that as general as they may seem, admittedly, these distinctions are real, and appreciating them can help you be more effective at communicating and inspiring changes in behavior.

  - Baby Boomers (born 1946–1964) are more likely to value structure, and frankly, at the age they are now may resist something they think of as silly or time-wasting. You will not find most of them doing yoga at their desks or taking a break to play games. They are, however, more structured and more likely to take an exercise class or go to the gym on a regular basis than some younger people.

  - Generation Xers (born 1965–1981) tend to have more of the characteristics of Baby Boomers if they were born early in this period or of Millennials if they were born later. Gen Xers are not as structured as Baby Boomers, nor as socially connected as the Millennials. They may need the most encouragement and modeling to change behaviors.

- Millennials aka "Gen Y" (born 1982–2004), are very socially connected and less structured, and often have a harder time fitting into what they see as the constraints of an office or business environment. Obviously, we're not talking about the younger end of this group; they're still in middle school. This is the group for which the foosball table in the cafeteria was designed. With this group, you may be more likely to have to rein them in than encourage them to take breaks.

So, before we move on, how about you take a walk around the block, stretch, climb that rock wall I put up over by the Red Bull machine, or whatever works for you? That's recreation, and in addition to adding a little fun and variety to your day, it will also help you concentrate on the important business at hand: how play can make you more effective in business.

The Power of Playing Alone

Even being pack animals, as humans are, the need and desire to be alone is often very strong. How many times have you asked a co-worker what they're doing for a night or weekend and heard, "I'm just going home and shutting the door"? This is a completely natural impulse, and like the craving for a specific type of food, is at times an absolute necessity. Especially in the contemporary work environment, where so much emphasis is placed on teamwork and group activity and collaboration, it's easy to get overwhelmed by the constant onslaught of information and interaction and sensory stimulus, whether directly or indirectly related to job function.

In many work environments, this can, and often does, take the form of too many meetings, so many demands on one's time, and a steady bombardment of input, whether in-person or electronic. And that's just some of the work-related stuff. Socializing in the office, politics, personal demands during the day, and more all come into play. In today's world, people are simply not able to segment their lives into work time and non-work time, try as they might. One of the problems we hear from people in business all the time is the many ways their attention is diverted from tasks at hand—and the stress that causes.

In terms of play, this is akin to being in a never-ending playgroup where the level of stimulus keeps a child on full alert at all times. As humans, we're simply not made to function on that level at all times, and indeed even in play groups, we consistently observe that one or two children, always dependent on the size of the group, may pull back or play alone during that time. This can be construed as either anti-social or indicative of a child's not being accepted by the group. Too often we see, particularly at the kindergarten level, an adult rush in and try to "fix" the situation, which can be at once disruptive to the dynamic of what's going on and confusing to the child who has actually absented him- or herself from the activity by conscious choice.

Moreover, in today's culture in the United States, children seldom have time to be alone, and this is most pronounced among more affluent sectors of the culture. Children are shuttled from activity to activity, and what suffers is unstructured time. Parents live in fear that either the unaccompanied child is vulnerable to danger, as author and blogger Lenore Skenazy points out in her book *Free-Range Kids* and her writings, or it assumed that there is something negative about being alone.

Assuming that there are no underlying psychological or social problems, solitary endeavors, and particularly solitary playtime, is as essential to healthy development as an ability to function within a group. So why is solitary playtime so often avoided with today's children? If you're a Baby Boomer, you probably remember significant blocks of time when you were unsupervised, but in today's world that's virtually gone. In large measure the constant attention to doing things and "being productive" is created by the idea that downtime is wasted time. Today's parents are very often driven to make sure that everything a child does is toward a specific end. If children are going to get into the best schools, compete effectively, and win, they need to be managed and guided and shaped and molded. As a result, consider in our current culture how many things children are engaged in that are run by an adult expert. The goal is not the exploration of something or having time with one's own thoughts and imaginations because that isn't "helping them get anywhere," which as we'll see in a moment is an illusion. Instead, the focus is on resume-building and the mastery of specific skills, whether in dance, sports, test-taking, or any other discipline. School time and after-school time are consumed to the point that every moment is scheduled. Summer vacation time, as well, for many kids is filled with activities, classes, and experiences. When we interview parents, there is either a misunderstanding or rejection of how important it is that children have unstructured time. And they live in fear of a child saying, "I'm bored." (My mother's response to that statement was always a crisp, "No, you're not. You've got a room full of books, all of outdoors, your bike, and your brothers. Figure it out.")

All of this, in many segments of the culture, leaves virtually no time for kids to be alone and left to their own devices, as the saying goes. The challenge is that they ultimately don't know how to be on their own or draw on their resources, which can leave them stressed out and ill prepared for a workforce that balances both group and solitary play, as it were.

What's the effect of this? For one, we have interviewed many managers who indicate frustration with some of their younger employees. Though these young workers may be very smart and very accomplished, they have a hard time functioning without constant direction. They are perfectly capable of doing tasks as assigned, but they need guidance and oversight at every step of the way, and they have been habituated to look for—and expect—feedback and validation at every step of the way. This certainly causes frustration with older managers and especially those who like to manage by exception—in other words, give an assignment and not have to figure out how it is accomplished. Now, of course, we're talking about somewhat extreme cases, and these young people certainly can and do learn to function effectively in these business environments, but the need for constant engagement is changing the dynamics of management in some companies. This is endemic as well in companies that have cultures driven by meetings and reliance on collaboration. In fact, for many of the managers we interview, the need for constant engagement, direction, and reinforcement is the new reality. One senior executive said, "These kids—we call them 'kids,' though they're adults—are often not able to function without their managers being more involved. Certainly, they are not as self-reliant as I was when I was starting out." What this means is not that one way is right or one is wrong, but there's a new reality that needs to be accommodated. It's understandable that there are levels of frustration, but inter-generational problems in the workplace are nothing new. So rather than fretting about it, perhaps it's time for managers to consider balancing the need for attention and reinforcement with more time for solitary play. After all, it's not like these things can't be learned after childhood.

But going back to understanding the importance of solitary play, consider its benefits and the important developmental functions it serves in childhood. Solitary play—without the constant bombardment of stimuli—overall helps children locate and identify themselves in the context of a group or a culture. This is absolutely necessary for social survival. On the individual level, solitary play fosters imagination, self-reliance, experimentation, information-processing, decision-making, and testing. This is well understood among play theorists and educational psychologists, but not so well understood among parents.

Becoming Part of the Group

None of us are born with knowledge of how we fit into a culture. Indeed, even the most rudimentary understanding of anthropology indicates that from the earliest days, children have to be socialized into a culture and cultural practices. From instruction to modeling and mostly through observation, children learn the essential lesson of survival in a group. As children get older and begin to be socialized outside the home, observation becomes one of the primary ways children learn to integrate themselves into a social structure. This observation is critical, as it allows the child to have an individual sense of self and project him- or herself into the group before actually participating. This can make some parents uncomfortable because they're afraid the child is hanging back and won't participate.

Let me give you one example: Observing her child at a play group sitting out of the group activity and watching, one parent assumed there was something wrong with her child—that she wasn't comfortable or fitting in. Actually, something else entirely was going on: The child, who was a few months younger than the other kids in the group (a huge difference in children versus adults), was actively observing everything that was going on. All the while, the child was gathering information, understanding the group dynamics, and trying to decide how to interact successfully. In order for the child to be accepted, it's imperative to learn how the group functions, and that only happens through observation. To bring it down to an elemental level, fitting into the pack and its structures is critical to survival. Thus, the time to observe and process how the group works is critical to success.

You may have seen this work for both good and bad in an office situation as people are brought into the pack or rejected from it. A new manager who doesn't take time to figure out the lay of the land and who doesn't work with the established systems, whether explicit or implicit, is likely to have a difficult time in management. The natural tendency for people is to resist change until such point as its necessary.

A new manager, the ink barely dry on his MBA, was brought into a toy company to modernize a legacy brand and expand its categories. Sales were strong and consistent, and the brand was profitable. In fact, sales in the previous year had been significantly up over the previous year. Certainly there were new opportunities, and the new corporate owners wanted to "modernize" the brand—not, it should be pointed out, based on research but because of the personal opinion of one of the new owners. Many of the people involved had spent many years in the toy industry and had insights into the sometimes peculiar ways it worked. In his very first meeting with the various department heads who would be reporting to him, however, the new vice president gave a scathing review of the current state of the business and announced wholesale changes. Not surprisingly, this didn't go over too well. He was seen as an aggressor who threatened the stability of the pack, which very naturally made people defensive and resistant. The vice president ultimately didn't last in the position and was resisted, albeit covertly, pretty much across the board. This was exacerbated by an attitude of superiority and condescension to virtually everyone who reported to him. Ultimately, the business was saved and successfully expanded by the second-in-command, who had been promoted from within and who knew who to work within the dynamics of the group. Ironically, the "solution" was to update the look of the product and the packaging, which was part of the regular line review process.

We've collected many versions of this story from different workers and middle managers over the years. But the point is, just like the child who observes a group before diving in, effective managers understand that they are entering into a human situation first and a business situation later. Early in my career, I worked for a publisher named Larry Danziger. In meeting after meeting he stressed the importance of treating people well. His catchphrase was "Your business goes up and down in your elevator every day," which of course means that your business is in large measure your people, and managing those dynamics is as important as managing your P&L. One of the pivotal moments in *A Christmas Carol* is when Scrooge realizes that he and his fellow apprentices would have done anything for their boss Fezziwig, not because he lavished money on them but because he led them with an acknowledgment of them as humans. In fact, Scrooge's epiphany is that it was not something tangible but an attitude and a set of behaviors that created value.

This is important to remember not just when you are new to a situation, especially when you're brought in over other people but with anyone who is new to a situation. People need time to observe and adapt. This was brought home to us in our own business with a new hire who had all the skills and work ethic we needed, and was doing an excellent job getting acclimated to the professional skills. He worked very well on his own, but when anything collaborative came up, he tended not to engage with the group, which created a problem in the more creative elements of the business. About a month into his employment, he spoke up in a brainstorming meeting and was not only directly on point, but very funny. (Appropriate humor is something we always value and enjoy.) He got a lot of approbation for his participation, and that was a turning point in his work. He has become a vital part of our business and a highly valued employee. Taking the time to find his way and understand, either consciously or unconsciously, the dynamics of relationships, the office hierarchies, and himself within the context of our organization gave him the tools he needed to succeed as a member of the team. Some peers and colleagues said, "He's come out of his shell." It's important as a manager to recognize this is a natural process—as natural as a child in the first days of kindergarten. Like a good parent, the savvy manager is attentive to the interactions among his employees, facilitating and supporting when necessary, and also knowing when to allow the process to take its time. We'll discuss the value of group play later.

Imagination

As we've been discussing in other chapters, the imagination is the source of all play. It is the source of all creativity and most like magicians or the gods in that it creates a reality out of thin air.

In solo play for kids, the imagination is where they are the most free and, in many respects, the most powerful. In imaginative play, kids are freed from the constraints of their world—the parents, teachers, and activities that control so much of their daily lives—and allowed to pursue wherever their thoughts take them. This does not happen out of context, however. It happens within the context of culture, knowledge, parental modeling, and the accumulated information at whatever age the child is.

Unlike imaginative play within a group, where the child is contributing to something larger than him or her, in solo play the child is in complete control. He or she doesn't also have to negotiate a group dynamic, which can have a significant impact on the experience.

If, as we suggest, play serves three functions—exploration, experience, and expression—solo imaginative play is where the expressive function finds its life. At the same time, play is always a reflection of its time, as are toys. The function of this play is to prepare children to enter the adult culture, and even if it is fantastical—as with superhero play—it is generally grounded in the larger *zeitgeist*, as perceived by the child and refracted through the imagination.

Talk to many Baby Boomer boys about their play, and you'll hear about a period in the early to mid-1960s when imaginative play centered on being secret agents. This was inspired by shows like *The Man From U.N.C.L.E.*, which in turn were inspired by the realities of the Cold War. The secret agent was a powerful and resourceful figure, usually in a black turtleneck—the perfect boys' fantasy. Seeing themselves as secret agents made them special and powerful. The feelings engendered were as real as if they actually happened, and the play was the catalyst, facilitating experiences that might be outside the daily reality of the child, where there's always an adult dictating parameters on behavior and guiding activity.

In the grown-up world, one of the best examples of imagination in solo play is the athlete visualizing something before actually doing it.

This is nothing other than play, pure and simple. It allows the athlete to have an experience of running the course, sinking the putt, or whatever. The benefit is that having done it in the imagination, the mind and the body already have had the experience, so that when the athlete does it in the real world it's not entirely new. In other words, by the time you have to do something, you've already done it, and there are few predictors of success as reliable as experience.

You probably already do this, whether you're planning your day, thinking about how an interaction with a co-worker or employer will go, and so forth. As adults, we call it planning, but really, it's nothing more than imaginative play.

In practice in business, however, we find that imaginative play often gets short shrift. Why this happens is not completely clear. Anecdotally, we find that time pressures and demands lead people to shortchange preparation. The idea that this saves time is not borne out by our interviews. Rather than spending the time preparing, some people we spoke to instead spend the time stressing. Lying awake at night worrying about a presentation for which you feel ill prepared is not a good, or productive, use of time.

Moreover, this is not something that others can do for you, which is why this is really solo play. The idea that spending time being imaginative is wasted is one of the real problems of our current business climate. Imagination is productive when it's focused and intentional. Just as in children, it builds confidence because, by the time a situation is "for real," you have experienced as much as you can from your perspective, which in turn allows you to be able to respond to those things that are outside your control. Going back to the secret agent play, part of the fun of the fantasy was always imagining the unforeseen challenges that you had to overcome and, because you were the hero in your imagination, overcoming them.

One way to think of the essential power of the imagination is in the difference between a map and a GPS device. Before the advent of the GPS, if you were taking a trip, you looked at a map and saw the route in your mind. In other words, you imagined where you were going in the context of the overall geography. Those little squiggles on a piece of paper became part of the information you were working with so that when you were actually driving, you knew where you were in context and where you were headed. In other words, you had a sense of the totality of the project of getting from point A to point B. With the GPS, you give over that visualization/play/preparation process to a machine. Yes, you may get where you're going, but you're doing so in response to a technology that directs you, so your engagement is different. You may not know the context of the surrounding area, so if, as happened to me in Georgia, the GPS wants to take you down a dirt road or doesn't know a road is closed, you are at the mercy of the technology to get you out of it. Don't get me wrong: I love the GPS, particularly in Washington, DC or LA, but I also generally like to look at the map so I have an idea of where I'm going.

It may seem counter-intuitive to some, but allowing time that could appear to be non-productive, as in, not about taking direct action to produce something tangible, but particularly in creative fields, the time for imagination can be highly productive. It also requires patience because the process, if fully engaged in, takes time. Linda Kraus-D'Isa, who owns a small, successful marketing consulting firm, describes one of her early bosses, who was a great believer in providing the room for people to use their imaginations: "We would have a meeting to go over a project, and then we'd see one of my co-workers sitting in his office with his feet up, staring into space. In other work environments, that might have been a reason to get fired. Depending on the person, it might have been a reason to get fired in that office. However, my colleague would eventually emerge with some of the best and most successful ideas for programs—programs that ultimately took shape in ways that were very similar to what was imagined."

Just as one other example of the efficacy of the imagination in the adult world, in the process of addiction recovery, the imagination is crucially important to people who are successful at it. When there is the urge to take a drink or drug, people are encouraged to use their imaginations to follow through to what will happen if they do. In most cases, this dredges up memories of unfortunate—if not catastrophic— outcomes and can be a governor of behavior. The imagination can be a literal lifesaver.

Just as with kids, information, context, objectives, and a willingness to follow ideas through to various conclusions are what imaginative play is all about. Most importantly, it doesn't cost anything—other than time—and it can be enormously empowering and beneficial to a work environment both in terms of actual ideas generated and the creative contributions individuals can make.

Self-Reliance, Experimentation, and Testing

I've put these three components together because they are closely interrelated. For children, play is an essential part of building self-confidence. In particular, unstructured free play allows children to draw on all of their experience and imagination to create, well, whatever they like. Mostly, though, this kind of play gives children the confidence that they can solve problems, from babies figuring out how to put a piece into a shape sorter up to school age and beyond when toys become more complex and they can figure out how to put together a LEGO set, for example. And failure is an important part of this process, as is overcoming that failure.

Broken down into its component parts, this type of play can really be stated as: analysis, action, and assessment. You can substitute "experimentation" for "action," or "testing" for "assessment." For a small child, naturally, this is a mostly subconscious process, and it happens very quickly. Just watch a baby unable to reach for something he or she wants and then get that quizzical expression before trying to figure out another way to achieve the goal, which can result in Mom racing to save the fragile item from Grandma's coffee table (but that's another story).

Still, this process is an important building block of learning and is in its own right a fundamental part of creating new experiences, as each success lays the foundation for future successes and builds the confidence to handle ever more complex problems and processes.

In the adult world, and particularly in business, we don't always get the kind of fast response to our actions a curious infant gets, so the process from experimentation to results takes time. But the principle still applies. In many smaller companies, there is so much pressure to get things done that the tendency is to jump from one item on the checklist to the next without taking the time to determine what happened and make adjustments. Particularly in today's world, business is dynamic, and changes happen quickly. Being able to respond to changing conditions is key. Here, however, we want to make the distinction between a response and a reaction. This may seem like a semantic difference at first, but in reality it is anything but.

Reactions are unconscious. Someone startles you and you flinch. A person tosses something to you unexpectedly and you automatically reach to catch it. Someone snaps at you and you snap back. These generally come out of our instinctive need to protect ourselves and are programmed into us as defense mechanisms when we don't have time to think about something. Reactions are very useful in many situations. They can even be useful in business when you're assessing creative work, for example. They are less effective, however, with complex problems, personnel problems, and issues that require more thought.

A response, on the other hand, takes more time, is generally more considered, and is a very conscious process. If a speeding car is bearing down you, you don't have time to consider options; you just get out of the way. If, however, you're trying to solve a personnel problem or create a branding strategy, that takes time.

Too often we observe business environments where there isn't the time for responses, and the corporate culture thrives on always being in a state of reaction. We've seen this in private companies and large corporations, and the effects can be damaging. Planning gets short-changed, and there are no opportunities for people to process information. They are forced into a system of constant reaction, or as one manager described it, "the never-ending fire drill." Generally, these situations have one common denominator: an owner or manager who doesn't trust his or her people and is always trying to control everything. As we've seen repeatedly, this is ultimately unsustainable, like the president of a large division of a consumer products company who would call his managers at midnight to say he disagreed with the choice of the color plastic for a minor part of a product. As any parent knows, part of building self-reliant kids is knowing when to step back and how to determine what's really important in any situation.

Fostering an environment that encourages solo play as we've been describing it has many benefits, from increased self-confidence to more active participation. Like the parent who tells the kid to go play outdoors, if you're going to be effective as a manager, it's wise to give your employees a chance to solve problems on their own. Few things are as de-motivating as micromanaging—unless it's being micromanaged. Empowered employees, like empowered kids, tend to be more creative, contribute more, and are more engaged.

The other benefit to creating an environment that fosters self-reliance is that it can foster greater creativity in group efforts, such as brainstorming. This doesn't come as any kind of surprise to people who study play. The child who is confident and reinforced in his or her problem-solving abilities, and as a result has a strong sense of individual identity, tends to make the transition to group play more easily.

Information Processing

Have you ever seen a baby surrounded by people all trying to play with him or her suddenly burst into tears? Or a preschooler in the midst of a playgroup suddenly start yelling? How about a slightly older child, after sitting at his or her desk in class all day, start to act out? To most adults, these seem like problems, and very often they interpret the event as the child being in the wrong. Too much of this, and an older child is seen as a behavior problem and sometimes even medicated. This is as unfortunate as it is unnecessary.

The problem is information overload—too much incoming stimulus and not enough time to process it. No wonder the synapses go haywire. Moreover, this is probably not a completely alien experience for you as an adult.

What solitary play does in this situation for kids is allows them to step back and process everything that's coming in. Kids have different abilities to process information, and individual kids have different thresholds for processing information. Solitary play allows them to shift their focus and sort through everything that's been coming in. This can be a subconscious process, much like data processing in the background, or it can be active.

Subconsciously, information, feelings, and so forth are essentially sorted and put into the context of previous experience. In a more active process, the child is trying to achieve the same result but through a play experience. This can be a story with action figures or dolls, gross motor play such as riding a bike, or simply running around or engaging in arts and crafts. The end result is that through solitary play, the child who has been challenged by a situation must process the information and add it to his or her every expanding wealth of experience.

Psychologist Jean Piaget was one of the pioneers of the theory that intellectual and biological development were interrelated. His work formed the basis for the theory of constructivism, which says that what children know is based on their experience. Thus, every new experience adds on to what has gone before to build knowledge out of what they experience and the ways in which they process or integrate that into their consciousness and personality. He suggested that learning has two component parts: assimilation and accommodation. Assimilation occurs when something new is incorporated into one's existing basis of experience, or frame of reference. Accommodation, on the other hand, occurs when what is known has to be adjusted to incorporate new information.

Piaget theorized that when a child encountered something outside his or her experience, it unbalanced perception—what he called "disequilibration." However, because as humans we naturally seek balance, also known as "equilibration," the challenge for the child is to integrate the new information to restore balance. As children become more mature, they become more adept at this and can handle greater and greater challenges, ultimately becoming habituated to the process of being thrown off balance and finding it again.

Piaget makes fascinating reading, and I'm a great believer in his theories, having observed them operating in children of many ages—as well as in adults. If you've ever said or heard someone say, "Well, that knocked me for a loop," you have firsthand knowledge of the process of disequilibration, and it goes on throughout life.

This process is highly individual, and constructivist theory rests on the premise that the individual must find his or her way back to equilibration based on the unique experiences that have shaped him or her. The thing about that is that it really must be done alone, and it takes time. By the time most people are adults, they are so accustomed to the process that it seems like second nature, as it should. Constructivist theory would hold that this process becomes almost automatic because it builds on what has gone before.

The downside, however, is what happens in many work situations where change comes so quickly and so often there really isn't time to integrate it. People we interview complain that the contemporary office environment is so changeable that there isn't any time to do anything but respond to changes. E-mails come pouring in steadily. Meetings consume hours and leave people exhausted. When this cycle keeps repeating and there isn't time for balance to be restored, it leads to declining productivity and burnout. Though burnout is an extreme, many professionals report that they are consistently overwhelmed with new information, and there is no time between meetings. In fact, middle managers at one company said that on any given day, they may have four to five meetings, each approximately an hour. This means that any independent work needs to happen outside of these times, which often means early mornings or late evenings, working through lunch, and so forth. In addition, they feel compelled to pay attention and respond to e-mails and texts at all hours of the day or night. This is not a particularly new observation; it's been analyzed in business articles for several years, certainly since the first years of this century when the BlackBerry was introduced and delivered e-mail to purses and pockets any time. The launch of the iPhone in June 2007 accelerated the pace, and today there is virtually no worker at any level who doesn't have 24/7 access to incoming communication. That's a lot of stimulus.

At the same time, the smartphone has created an atmosphere in which workers feel they need to be accessible 24/7, and indeed "fear of being out of the loop" is something that keeps middle managers especially feeling the need to respond to every buzz and beep. This attitude in business has trickled down even to kids, and the very real phenomenon of "FOMO" (fear of missing out). Partially driven by social media, which people check obsessively even when they're not receiving inbound communication, it's possible in today's world never to be cut off from the incessant stimulus of the outside world.

When we talk to managers and workers, many of them attribute their stress levels to the pace of business. Well, business is going to stay fast, and if recent years are any indication, it's just going to get faster. Yet it's not the pace of business that we think is creating the stress, or even the amount of information that is coming in; it's the lack of time to—in Piaget's terms—either assimilate or accommodate what's coming in. This constant bombardment of stimuli creates a level of stress on our systems that keeps us in a constant state of alertness and preparedness. We are constantly responding to one thing after another, and especially if there is an emotional component brought on by such issues as FOMO, we are constantly working at elevated adrenal levels, which is exhausting.

One of the examples I use when I speak to groups about this is the lion in the wild. In pursuit of a wildebeest snack, the lion exerts maximum energy and all its strength in capturing and killing its prey. Sated, however, it is content to sit in the sun for hours, without exerting any energy. And, while the Discovery Channel and Animal Planet may feature dramatic video of lions attacking their prey, in fact, only about 50 percent of their diet is gotten this way. The rest if from scavenging, a relatively low-impact activity. Lions have an instinctual ability to use energy as needed and as appropriate. More importantly, when they are not called upon to use that energy, they don't. Instead they rest and recharge. You can observe this in virtually any species. (Well, I'd except ants, having had an ant farm on my desk for quite a while that seemed to put me to shame when I would daydream. Ants seem to work non-stop all day long—at least until they collapse and die. I recommend the ant farm as a cautionary tale.)

The other example I like to point to is torture. The practices employed in the Abu Ghraib prison or at the Guantanamo Bay detention camp included non-stop stimulation. Over-exposure to light and noise was designed to provoke sensory overload. Although this can in no way be condoned, and I shudder at seeming to minimize the gravity of the situation, these practices purported to achieve results by wearing people down and essentially short-circuiting their systems so that their emotional and intellectual facilities were undermined.

I do not want to minimize the suffering these prisoners underwent in any way, but I use it as an extreme example of what can happen to the human body when exposed to such extremes. The adrenal system is overtaxed and given no time to recover, and I do want to suggest that by keeping ourselves in a constant state of alert, we are, to a certain degree, torturing ourselves. The body doesn't know if your life is actually threatened or if you've forgotten to return a phone call. The chemical reaction is the same: Adrenaline goes pumping into the system. Over time, the body becomes accustomed to these heightened levels, and the drop, rather than the constant rise, in them becomes the issue of concern. At that point, the emotions kick in and there is fear that people aren't doing enough, and the cycle continues. Ultimately, it's possible to become addicted to adrenaline, and as with any addiction, untreated it will ultimately ravish the body.

If you question this is happening as part of our culture, look around. Walk down the street in New York City any day and any time, and you'll see people tapping away on their screens. Go to a Broadway show, and at intermission (and sometimes during the show, maddeningly), you'll see screens lit up with people either working or posting to social networks. Sit in any meeting and observe individuals tapping away on their devices while someone is presenting. Aside from being rude, this scattered focus stresses our systems and is ultimately counter-productive because there is no time for the brain to store and sort the information. Going back to Piaget, it all comes in, and because so much is coming in, the brain doesn't know whether to assimilate or accommodate, and as a result it is not perceived as important and often discarded. Have you ever said to someone, "But we went over that in the meeting"? That's the impact of too much information and not enough time to process. That's one reason we have a policy of no referring to devices in meetings, with the exception of referring to calendars as part of a scheduling discussion. What we find is that meetings are shorter, are more focused, and lead to more concrete action steps—and need less repetition, aside from a meeting report.

Interestingly enough, humans are really the only species that can override the natural process of information processing that leads to the kind of problems outlined above. In our experience, it's largely ego-driven, and it dates back millennia. Known as anthropocentrism, the idea is that human beings are superior to every other animal on the planet, and the person who thinks he's a superior human can be incredibly insufferable to work for. (Admit it: You know more than a few of these.) The problem, of course, is that this sense of superiority is little more than an opinion, but like any belief it's powerful enough to alter the natural process of information processing. In simple terms, we tend to see and hear what we want to that coincides with our opinions. This is not to completely short-circuit Piaget, but it sure makes it harder to learn.

A few years ago, I was giving a presentation at a conference, and I looked out in the audience and saw one of the participants tapping away on his e-mail. At this point, I've become conditioned to that; it happens all the time. However, at the dinner that night, I happened to be seated across from the guy who had been working on his device.

I said, to him, "I noticed that you were working on your phone throughout the whole presentation. Why was that?"

He said, without a trace of irony, "When I attend a presentation, I give the speaker 30 seconds to get my attention, and if he doesn't, I figure there's really nothing I can learn."

"Really?" I replied. "So your employer gave you four days to attend this conference; paid for your travel across the country, your hotel, and meals; and you believe that each of these speakers, some of whom are people I've been excited to hear, gets only 30 seconds to prove themselves to you?"

"Yes."

Now, setting aside that it's virtually impossible to set up the subject of a presentation in 30 seconds, we also have the problem of information processing that takes a bit longer than that. I mention this case because it is extreme and, in my experience, rare, and had more to do with one individual's opinions than a failure of communication. But the extreme illustration shows how one's ego can both shut down the process of information processing but the reception of information at all.

For an intellectual proposition, it takes a bit of time and concentration to determine whether or not one is going to assimilate or accommodate the information, and that happens in the subconscious. After the experience just described, I toyed with the idea of being shot out of a cannon into a stream of fireworks surrounded by the Rockettes as a way of opening future presentations, but the logistics seemed daunting and, fortunately, largely unnecessary.

Here's the thing: We can make snap, pre-conscious decisions in an instant, what we discussed earlier as reactions. That's the basis for virtually all advertising and what passes for political discourse in our current culture. A reasoned response takes time, and we need to give it that time.

When kids get overwhelmed and act out, we give them a time out. We separate them from all the stimuli, and give them a chance to calm down and process what's happening. Adults need that too, but we seldom give ourselves a time out—even when we need one. Build in time for recovery.

	What You Can Do
1.	Give people space and time. One of the biggest inhibitors of productivity we see constantly is that there is not time to process information—that is, analyze and plan based on the scope of a project. Build that into your schedule, along with clear directives, responsibilities, and action steps. Then give people the time to do their jobs.
2.	Make more of meetings. Ensure that your meetings are streamlined, are resolution- and action-oriented, and involve only the people you need. Don't schedule full days of meetings, if you can possibly avoid it. After a while you get diminishing returns in terms of people's attention and investment.
3.	Respect non-working time. Give people a chance to walk away from business. We always tell people there is no difference in the business world between 5 p.m. one day and 9 a.m. the next. If you're a manager, don't expect your people to be on call 24/7. Are they really going to be getting things done in that time? If you *must* write e-mails in the middle of the night, put them in your outbox and send in the morning. Take the time at night to walk away from work, change your focus, and allow the subconscious to do its job of processing all the information from the day. If you must, write notes of things that occur to you, but don't refer to them again until the next day.

What You Can Do (continued)

4.	Ban cell phones from meetings. Not only is it considerate of the other people in the meeting, you don't want to be distracted by too much stimulus that fragments your concentration. And don't tell me you're "multi-tasking." That's a myth, anyway. You are simply shifting your concentration from one thing to the next, regardless of how rapidly you are doing it. Why do people have traffic accidents when they're texting and driving? Because their attention is not on the driving, even for a few seconds. Be present to the issue at hand. It really is more efficient, and you don't get people resenting you for wasting their time.
5.	Move a muscle. There's a reason kids get recess, and the loss of recess is a serious problem in our educational system right now. It contributes to all kinds of behavioral and attention problems. The reality is, you're not a brain in a jar. You have a body, and it has all kinds of chemical processes going on that affect mood, attention, and health. Moving and being physical, as with kids and as described earlier, allows you to metabolize the chemicals that are released do to stress and other issues. It also gives your mind a break so that the subconscious sorting and categorizing of all the inputs can take place. I'm not suggesting you take two hours a day to work out, but I am saying that it's important to acknowledge our physical needs throughout life. People who sit all day shorten their hip flexors. People with hip flexor issues often get back issues. People with back issues are in pain and miss work. You see how it goes. We're physical creatures. Be physical.

The Benefits of Group Play

How familiar are you with this scene, or a variation of it?

Tom and Billy, ages 2 or 3, are happily playing side by side and virtually ignoring one another, a fairly common form of "parallel play" at this age. Suddenly, for whatever reason, Tom decides that he "needs" the truck that Billy is playing with and snatches it away. Tears ensue. Sometimes a brawl. The truck may or may not be used as a weapon. Even if no one is bruised, neither child is happy. Suddenly an adult steps in, breaks up the argument, and says, "You have to learn to share." (This scenario works with girls and their toys as well.)

Although that may quell the argument for a moment, don't be surprised if Billy and Tom have no idea what to do with this directive, at least initially, and will probably look at each other confusedly and go back to what they were doing. Their attention will have shifted, but they are not relating to one another.

Developmentally, children still see themselves in isolation at this age and have no idea how to relate to others. When they get slightly older, perhaps around age 4, they may engage in what's called "associative play," in which both children are playing independently but engaged in the same activity, whether trucks or dress-up or whatever.

It is only later that children begin to play cooperatively, at ages 4 or 5. This begins to occur because at that age their development has progressed to the point where they are verbal, able to communicate likes and dislikes, and able to share ideas and begin to experience benefits of playing with other children.

The process for children from seeing themselves in isolation to seeing themselves in the context of a group is a developmental process that evolves as they gain abilities. Yet it is also one that has to be taught. In other words, though children may, in fact, become more inclined to interact in a group setting, they must also be socialized to do so within the context of the culture they live in. For example, there may be specific rules governing the interaction between boys and girls, between children and adults, and so forth. As in all cultural learning, what is explicitly told to children and modeled for them are the patterns and practices they are most likely to adopt.

It's important to understand the interaction of physical and mental development in concert with socialization as the central elements of developing effective—and productive—group play. With children, it takes a lot of engagement. For instance, in the conflict scenario previously described, unless the adult remains involved in the ongoing interaction and demonstrates or describes what is appropriate behavior, the conflict may stop, but that doesn't mean anything has been learned. We often observe that after an admonition to "play nice," the conflict is stopped, and for all intents and purposes, the intervention will have been considered a success. However, it's important here to note that stopping conflict is not the same as achieving a resolution. There has been no, for want of a better word, systemic change, and it's likely that the scene with Billy and Tom will repeat again.

Why?

Because there is no clear, positive incentive for them to change their behavior other than in the short term. In other words, only when Billy or Tom perceives that the individual benefit he will derive from sharing, and by extension engaging in a group, is greater than the benefit of repeating a previous action will he have a motivation to change. (Of course, there are variables that make one child more likely to share than another, but the basic principle is unchanged.)

Thus, if Billy and Tom ultimately begin to share effectively, it can be assumed that they are doing it out of self-interest. Over time and as a result of experience, the child begins to understand sharing in a larger context and develops the capability to determine when to share, or when not to. This sharing is the fundamental component of group play, and it's critical to creating an integrated child who functions effectively within a social structure. There are some assumptions in this, notably that we are dealing with an emotionally stable child who is beginning to develop a set of healthy boundaries.

Whether or not sharing is innate or learned, at least as relates to preschool children, has been the subject of a variety of different studies with differing conclusions. Some recent studies conclude that children will naturally engage in sharing without intervention from a very young age when there is a tangible, emotional, or otherwise identifiable reward associated with that sharing. This certainly makes us feel better about our natures, doesn't it?

These studies also seem to challenge the conventional wisdom that humans are intrinsically selfish and need to be socialized into considering others. The flaw with these studies, whatever they conclude, however, is the inability to control for other influences on a child such as personality or the home environment. As with many studies dealing with children (and adults, for that matter), it's impossible to eliminate all external influences and get an unalloyed result, no matter how big your sample is. To do this, one would have to create a human being raised with no outside stimuli who could only be used for one study before he or she was compromised. You'd be right to think this sounds like some kind of dystopian, science fiction scenario. In other words, we're never going to be able to demonstrate empirically and unequivocally where sharing comes from. Better yet, for our purposes it doesn't really matter.

In fact, let's assume for our purposes that even if a predisposition to share is an inherent human trait, effective sharing and group play is a learned behavior. Moreover, it's something that needs to be practiced over time. Essentially, Billy and Tom have to learn *how* to share, *why* they should, and what's in it for them individually.

Let's take the previous hypothetical situation one step further and suppose that over time, after their first interaction around age 2, Tom and Billy become best friends and as they get a little older discover the pleasures of interactive, associative play. As noted, this is something that usually occurs naturally as kids develop and find themselves interacting with others. Around the age of 4 or 5, kids begin to acknowledge others, are influenced by them in their play, and at the same time discover they can influence others. This is also the time when kids are starting to separate from parents and begin developing an individual identity, which finds expression in co-play.

At this point, the sharing begins to have evident, direct, and tangible social and psychological benefits, so—no surprise—kids jump on it. From this point on sharing and interaction become essential parts of play and interaction, and, significantly, children begin to develop a sense of themselves as individuals *and* as individuals within the context of a group. Sharing, group interaction, and by extension, *not* sharing become some of the ways that children exert power both for themselves and over others. I'm guessing you can see where this is going.

Before we get there, however, let's take a look at the benefits of group play:

- Trust.
- Interaction.
- Companionship.
- Common purpose.
- Support.

Trust

Before Tom is going to let Billy play with his truck willingly, he has to believe that giving up his total control of the truck and allow another person to have part of that control is going benefit him. This is a tough concept for preschool kids, and as is trust in adults, it's developed over time. When the outcomes are consistently positive, and the payoffs of fun and companionship are present, sharing becomes pleasurable.

If, on the other hand, Tom shares the truck with Billy and Billy takes it away, conflict is inevitable. Tom feels violated and may have a hard time sharing with others in the future. As difficult as this is, it's an important milestone for kids, however, because they begin to learn discernment of who they can count on and who they can't.

Interaction

Interaction is a key component of group play and sharing, precisely because there are other people in the process. How effectively kids interact with others, their success at those interactions and the context of behavior and perception they build as a result of those interactions is both formative in terms of personality development and essential in terms of negotiating play and school lives.

In the past 15 years, really since about 1999 with the advent of a lot of reading toys, there has been a great deal of emphasis placed on the knowledge that kids have when they enter kindergarten. This is a follow-up to various fashions regarding kids "reading" at a very early age or being able to demonstrate some other level of academic accomplishment. This even extended to the now-debunked notion that playing classical music to newborns or babies in the womb somehow facilitated more sophisticated brain development.

When I was entering preschool, one had to be able to dress oneself, be toilet trained, and know one's name. Though that may be a simplification for effect, today's kids are required to know the alphabet, basic numbers, and other academic subjects as a criterion for entering school.

However important in later school life this fundamental knowledge is, kindergarten is essential for kids to begin to negotiate and understand the group setting and to begin to build that foundation of successful interaction that is essential to living in a group-based society. This is one of the primary objectives of kindergarten, for kids to begin to develop the basic disciplines of being in a classroom setting, of learning in digestible amounts, and practicing behaviors they'll need in the primary grades. In blunt terms, the role of kindergarten is to tame kids so they'll be able to function in the school environment.

And that means learning to interact effectively. As kids become socialized into groups outside their families, they begin to learn the value of interaction with others, notably a peer group where they are, to some extent, on an equal footing in terms of power—versus a parent who controls virtually everything in their lives at that age. From common interests to joint creativity and problem-solving, kids begin to see themselves and their capabilities in a larger context.

Interaction also helps kids understand roles and boundaries as well as the multiple hierarchies they have to negotiate in groups and what's appropriate in each one. And of course, coping with different personalities. Learning how to negotiate these interactions for desired outcomes doesn't come naturally. Kids need to be socialized into appropriate interaction with one another. Kids don't inherently understand that what might be okay at home might not be at school, for instance.

This is essentially the message of the 1963 children's classic *Where the Wild Things Are.* If you haven't read it in a while, it's probably a good thing to pick up again and read with an adult's eyes. Originally banned because it showed a child behaving badly, it is now an established staple of children's literature. The hero, Max, after acting out and being sent to his room, imagines himself in a new world, where he is a major figure of fun and freedom. Ultimately, however, he discovers that in this world he is quite literally out of context and returns home to a hot supper and the embrace of his mother. As part of learning to be in a group, whether a family or a class, once they begin to understand the structural function of the group, children need to challenge that structure in order to fully understand where they fit in. Good parents and teachers allow kids to do this when they are causing no harm to themselves or others.

Learning to interact in the larger context, as with trust, helps children build a frame of reference for interpreting what goes on around them and also for understanding themselves in the context of a group or a relationship.

Companionship

Every social structure—family, school, office—thrives on interaction. One of the benefits of group play and sharing is always companionship. Whether it's the reinforcement of the like-minded or the challenges of someone who has a different opinion, companionship is one of the ways we create a circle of people we trust and we come to rely on.

In business, this is often called our network, and it's essential not just for when we need help with a job hunt or to get something done. Obviously, no one wants to go through things alone; that's part of human nature. Companionship helps reduce stress and gain perspective as well as reinforces one's identity either in one-to-one relationships or within a group.

Common Purpose

This is central to any effectively functioning group. For children, this can be a play scenario in which they have to cooperate to accomplish something. It can be a team, a choir, or virtually anything undertaken by two or more people. Children and young people who function well in groups all share one common trait: They are able to focus on the group objective rather than their own needs.

To effectively function in this type of environment, kids need to have a sense of themselves as individuals, and they need appropriate communication skills. At the same time, they also work best when there are clear objectives and they understand how their participation contributes to the whole. And one other thing about group work: Kids are very concerned about fairness, particularly as it relates to their willingness to put their personalities aside for the benefit of the group. This is a huge step for kids in their development that usually happens by around age 6, and it becomes an essential part of any of the collaborative learning process in most schools and later in business.

Support

The value of support is obvious, but it's important to define it as a component of group dynamics. When most people think of support with relation to kids and play, they think of validation—cheerleading or giving encouragement or positive feedback, or building self-esteem. It's all of that too, but support the way I'm using it here is not the altruistic commentary from someone outside the group (a parent, teacher, or friend, for instance), which is not always useful and sometimes is more effective at salving hurt feelings than anything more productive.

Support, as we define it, is an organic element of the group dynamic that helps the group to be more successful as a whole. In a group play context, support is about identifying and using the capabilities of the individual group members to achieve the common purpose. A great placekicker has a different set of skills than a linebacker, for example, but both of them are essential to the success of the team. In the few years that I danced, my best skill was that I could do the lifts. No one was going to look at me over the leading dancers, but I served a greater function to the group as a whole. We are not all equally gifted or even proficient, but the combination of capabilities in a group setting can be very powerful and make for an effective group.

Children learn in group play, always assuming that they are first aligned on common purpose, several critical lessons. First, they learn to assess their own skills in the context of a group and related to an objective. Second, they learn to assess the skill of others as related to the objective. And finally they learn to categorize these skills based on their observations. Combined with observations of behavior and inter-actions within the group, children are beginning to lay the foundation for cooperative interaction that they will need for any group situation in their lives. Effectively participating in a group gives children the opportunity to understand what they do best and bring it to the group, which in a group play situation can become very empowering for the child, especially when that knowledge is generated organically as a result of the group interaction.

Other Benefits of Group Play

As noted, the most productive group play for children is that which occurs without the supervision of an adult. Indeed, the presence of an adult, whether it's an expert or someone to monitor behavior, changes the dynamic entirely and undermines the value of the play. The focus shifts from a group dynamic to a group following one person.

Adults usually think that they are doing what's best for kids by teaching them important skills or keeping the peace, and those are important. At the same time, it's also important for a group to create its own identity without that overarching influence. It's no surprise, as we've discussed in the section on story, that the groups of children in literature—from Hogwarts to Narnia and beyond—need to function without the direct involvement of an adult.

The skills children learn in this situation are critical. One of the aspects of group play that is shortchanged when there is one arbiter or teacher is that the group tends not to be self-policing. This is a critical skill because learning to operate effectively within a peer group, and its dynamics and hierarchies are essential components of effective socialization. In terms of social development, the transition from parental control to functioning within a group is absolutely critical—and another one of the functions of kindergarten and early classroom education. Respect for peers, listening, assessing, and all of these life skills are critical because, at least hopefully, an integrated adult is going to have to function in groups for the majority of his or her life, and there are going to be many more peers with whom you will have to successfully interact than there are parents or parental figures, simplistic as that sounds.

In 1998, a card game called Pokémon became a phenomenal fad with grade- and middle-school children. Having certain cards became a kind of currency among kids, and trading these cards became a popular schoolyard activity. Children of this age, however, may not be the smartest negotiators and trades sometimes got out of hand, with "trader's remorse" setting in and feelings getting hurt. This led many schools to ban the cards and trading.

At the height of this fraught and feverish frenzy in 1999, I was talking to a parent whose son was distraught at having traded away a prized Charizard (one of the characters) card for cards that he ultimately thought had less value. In other words, he had made what, on reflection, he considered to be a bad decision. The school and other parents were adamant that the father reverse the trade. He refused; his son was beside himself, and the parents and teachers were upset. When I asked him why he refused to reverse the trade, he said, "A kid makes only one bad trade in his life. Better it should be this." This is, in my opinion, good parenting. Others may be outraged that their child had to experience frustration and disappointment as the result of his or her actions, but this is one of the prime functions of group play. The father's son had to come to terms with the consequences of his actions and continue to function within the peer group, and was smarter, one hopes, for it. These are things that can't be taught; they can only be experienced. All of us have events in our childhood like this that we can recall, and it can be an interesting exercise to trace that forward to your behavior or point of view today on that topic. When adults step in and try to rescue kids from negative feelings or consequences, they are basically robbing children of the opportunity to resolve the situation in themselves and go on. And they are only postponing the inevitable learning, which will have to happen at some point or other.

There is a lot of coverage of "helicopter parenting" and even "dive-bomber parenting," which keeps the parents involved in the minutiae of a child's life. At one point in 2006, I worked with a company that had a salesperson who called her father every time she had a setback. I've received calls from the parents of young people being considered for jobs. The temptation is always to be critical of this because "I wasn't like that when I was their age." Could there be anything more counter-productive? Doubtful. It's the reality of today's culture, and you're going to have to deal with it.

But it does mean, particularly if you're a Baby Boomer or someone who takes a more classically military approach to business, that you may have to adjust your management style. You may need to provide more feedback, more encouragement, and validation to understand the mindset and experience of people who were raised to get feedback and response constantly.

Group Play in Business

Whatever your function within a business, if you ever have to interact with more than one person, you're going to be faced with dealing with a group, and that means dealing with the many different personalities, issues, subtexts, and politics that are endemic in any kind of group activity.

Over the years, we observed characteristics of effective groups of all sizes in companies of all sizes. Groups that are subsets of groups overlap with other groups, and so on. Group play, on an adult level, is one of the defining characteristics of the contemporary company. Here are the components we consistently find make for the most effective and functioning business groups.

Respect

If you're trying to build or participate in an effective group, it's imperative that you respect the other members of the group. Although this seems incredibly obvious, it doesn't always happen in business environments. Groups, especially those that work together over time, tend to become a bit like families. That is, people make their assessments about the individuals, judge them, and either accept or discard ideas based on those judgments. This is human nature. Our biological programming is designed to make these determinations, and they're hard to stop. Your system is trying to tell you where you sit in the power structure, what the hierarchy is, who to mate with, who to eat. This is all programmed into our reptile brains, and you can't help it. This is both a good and a bad thing. On the positive side, you have an inherent ability to size people up based on observation and experience, which allows you to interact successfully with others based on this. On the negative side, we can either give too much power to people or discount them based on these judgments. In either scenario, this potentially unbalances the group dynamic, which ultimately can make the work more difficult. Fortunately, as mentioned previously, human beings also have the ability to override these reptilian proclivities, an ability that one assumes evolved specifically to help us survive and thrive within groups. In fact, one of the things we often tell people in companies is to leave their egos at the door. Don't take things too personally (always excepting egregious and obvious abuse, which is never acceptable) and try to assume that others want things to work as much as you do. This last note is important because in all the years of working with companies and interviewing individuals, we have yet to find someone who doesn't want to do a good job. Their personalities or skills may not be a match for the company or the project, but we have yet to find someone who doesn't want to do a good job.

You don't have to like someone to work effectively with them, though it can make for a more pleasant work environment. You do, however, need to respect what they bring to the table and their different skills. This is easiest when a group has a clearly defined common purpose, as we'll discuss.

Appreciate Differences in Thinking Processes

As noted, groups work most effectively when diverse skills and talents are understood and employed to achieve the common purpose. Over and above professional skills and experience, which hopefully complement one another in a group setting, it's important to realize that there are different thought processes inherent to each individual. Children have different play styles and learning styles, and that doesn't change as we get older. The challenge, especially for managers, is to determine these in each of your team members, and effectively balance and leverage them.

One of the best examples of the type of business where this difference is pronounced is the marketing or advertising agency. We've worked with many of them throughout the years, and they all have a very specific divide: creatives and account management. These can be contentious relationships for many reasons, but we believe that the prime cause is different ways of thinking—divergent and convergent.

In her book, *Sex, Lies & Creativity,* Julia Roberts describes the brain chemistry of divergent versus convergent thinking. It's an accessible description of a sophisticated process, and it's reassuring to know that this is part of who we are. In practice, however, it's something that needs to be addressed and accounted for managing and participating in a group.

Simply put, divergent thinkers, as the name implies, tend to consider issues broadly. They are often more conventionally creative in that they have an ability to consider many different factors in coming up with solutions. These are the people who in brainstorming meetings come up with the off-the-wall ideas because they are able to see similarities and relationships, however subtle, between diverse (hence, divergent) elements and ideas. They want the freedom to freely associate without structure and see where their ideas take them and consider all kinds of options, even some that might seem farfetched. You want these people on your team because they are the ones who will push the envelope and help push concepts to the next level.

Convergent thinkers, on the other hand, are more methodical and structural in their thinking. Again, we're simplifying, but these individuals want to take an established set of data or information and synthesize it into one concrete and defensible solution.

As you might imagine, when you put these two different types of thinkers together in a room, you're likely to have conflict. Each side is frustrated with the other and convinced that their way is correct. The fact of the matter is, though, both are essential. The divergent thinker feels constrained and limited by the convergent thinker, and the convergent thinker thinks the divergent thinker is all over the map and not focused on finding the "right" answer.

As mentioned, this conflict in thinking styles is most evident in agencies or situations where creative people and project managers have to work together on a daily basis, but it happens in virtually every kind of business. Moreover, these ways of thinking exist on a spectrum. An outstanding creative director, for example, is probably near the middle between these two types of thinking. He or she is most able to negotiate between the people who are further out toward their respective ends of the spectrum. In order to be effective and productive, a group needs both types of thinkers. You need the creative ideas, but you also need to implement them.

A well-functioning group can appreciate these differences and leverage them to their advantage. However, one of the best tips we have for people who need to function in a group is that when you're feeling frustrated with how someone is approaching an issue, that's a good time to take a step back and try to realize how the person you're annoyed with is approaching the problem. As with kids, an effective group is also self-policing and can identify when different skills are needed. We see this consistently in brainstorming sessions, and it's a good model to follow. The convergent thinkers (usually account management) lay out the challenge and the objectives, then step back and let the divergent thinkers (copywriters, art directors, producers) have at it. The convergent thinkers bring it all back to earth, the divergents embellish, and you're off to the client. This is no different from when kids draw on each other's talents to build the best possible solution.

I know this probably sounds obvious and even a bit simplistic, but when you strip away the personalities and politics that often influence the other dynamics of a group, it is simple, but it requires a willingness to, in the language of adolescents, get over yourself.

Common Purpose

You can also call common purpose "clear objectives," but what seems on the surface to be one of the most obvious components of any group is also one of the most often shortchanged, and this is true whether a group is convening for a meeting or a long-term project.

The group needs to be in agreement about what its goals are, or inevitably chaos ensues, perhaps not immediately (which might actually be a good thing to get you back on track) but inevitably, and the group will not be productive. At the same time, every smaller group must have a common purpose that serves the larger objectives of the company, or why create the group in the first place? Again, sounds simplistic, but too often we see companies that confuse action with accomplishment, as I like to say. We see this particularly in large companies. For example, the PR department of a large company recently planned an event for one of its flagship brands. It was a press event during a trade show, and a group was assembled from various parts of the company to plan logistics, creative materials, invitations, guest lists, and so forth. With a budget upward of $200K for a 3-hour event, it was a significant undertaking. The purpose of the group was to get the event designed and implemented. They achieved their objective.

However, there was one hitch: Nobody ever asked whether or not this was going to achieve the larger brand objectives, and did the appropriate analysis, before forming the group and setting off on the process. It was only later, with 3 weeks to go before the event, that senior management became aware that no one outside the brand team and other members of the company at the trade show were going to attend. The event was canceled because the finance group was able to determine that the cost of canceling was significantly less. Because the company was under scrutiny for its spending by Wall Street analysts at the time, this was the better course. It's important to note that the party planning group did nothing wrong. Rather, by all criteria they succeeded in terms of timing and budget. The problem was that no one asked the question as to whether this served larger company objectives at the time and for the cost involved.

Your common purpose is the benchmark against which you measure everything you do. It provides the checks and balances and the basis for analysis of ideas and actions to the extent possible, and as the example illustrates, in the context of your larger business objectives. In practice, your common purpose facilitates decision-making and focused action. If, as with an online company we worked with, the goal of a group was to increase traffic from a specific demographic, everything was reviewed with an eye toward that, as well as what the contribution of increasing participation of that demographic could mean to the company as a whole. Though there are never any guarantees that anything will work in business given all the inevitable variables, this clear focus means that it's easy to cull ideas that are off topic or would waste time. Just like the child who drops something when it doesn't work, assessing concepts against a common purpose lets you get on to the more productive play, as it were.

When setting a common purpose, or objectives, for your group, it's also important to define what success will look like and how you will determine that. Some results will be statistically quantifiable, which will please the convergent thinkers. These apply to outcomes that are specifically measurable, such as sales, traffic, customer turnover, and so forth. Others, however, may be a little more intangible, such as customer satisfaction or other squishy data that's virtually impossible to measure in isolation and for which there are no foolproof measurement methodologies.

It's important in what I'm calling "squishy data" areas to create meaningful benchmarks and not rush to apply metrics to everything.

Too often we see numbers used as a defense or a validation, but does anyone ask what those numbers mean? Are the hours employees spend on the job an accurate measure of productivity? Can you correlate the number of people who attend an event or see a YouTube video to increased sales? Probably not, because your audience is so diverse.

Speaking of, nowhere do we see metrics being misapplied more than in the world of social media. Yes, more and more people are watching YouTube, and many kids are watching more YouTube than broadcast TV in terms of hours. So lots of companies are pouring lots of money into trying to make videos that will "go viral." That's definitely a definable common purpose, but is it meaningful for your larger business objectives? If your goal is to build viewers, sure. If you're trying to sell product, it's not as clear.

For example, even when those videos are related to toys, as many are with the high popularity of "unboxing" videos (literally, people taking toys or other products out of boxes—go figure) in 2015, those numbers are not a reliable predictor of sales because many more kids watch those videos for the entertainment value than because they want the toys. This is great for the YouTube personalities, but we see many toy companies correlating views to demand. They in turn promote that to the retailers, who buy larger quantities, and in many cases end up stuck with product. This is just one example of how isolated metrics are not sufficient for projecting an outcome. But it's very common. Hey, you can tell your bosses, "We had 5 million views on YouTube; we all thought this was going to be big."

The other problem with developing a common purpose occurs when the stated purpose is not the real purpose. We see this happen primarily in small, entrepreneurial companies that are headed by someone with a forceful personality. This is more like the group of kids with an adult expert or teacher than a functioning, productive group as we've been describing it here, although it does occur, and for the sake of your career—and at times your sanity—you need to be aware of it. The stated purpose of the group, or the company, may be to grow sales or be successful in a specific industry, but in practice the real common purpose is to gratify the ego and the changing directions of the person who's really running the show. This is a person who, whatever else he or she might say, is not really interested in forming a functioning company, let alone groups within that company, but rather is so convinced that his way is right that it frustrates everyone who works for the company, unless they are happy to serve that particular master and accept the limitations that come with it.

I worked with a senior manager who had been relocated to take a job in such a company. He had an impressive track record of building sales, established success in the business, and was asked to come on board to take the company to the next level. Promises of a presidency and even a future CEO position and equity in the company all proved too good to resist. However, the reality turned out to be something else entirely. The company was providing the owner with a significant income, the investments the new executive wanted were denied, and he found himself at the mercy of someone with no boundaries who would call at all hours, insist on travel at a moment's notice, shake up departments without consulting the person who was supposedly in charge, and change directions and cancel products even as production was about to start. For this particular executive, who happens to be a fairly strong convergent thinker, this was madness.

Moreover, in talking with the people who had been at this company a while, they were complacent and not looking for change. Their common purpose, in a small Midwestern town, was to keep their jobs and not make waves. You know, there's nothing wrong with that, and working at that company afforded many of those people a lifestyle they were comfortable with. However, for our executive, who was more ambitious and was aiming for a C-suite job, his attempts to shake the place up and put it on a more traditional growth path never got anywhere. In fact, he faced a political challenge and pushback from day one—which is exactly what happens when the real common purpose is unstated, obscure, or something else entirely from what one thinks it is.

This is why in business, developing a common purpose is a bit more complex than children saying "Let's build a fort" or some such. But its effect on the outcome of any project is just as real. Once the fort is the stated objective, anything that doesn't contribute to its construction should be jettisoned. In business, of course, the process includes a lot more analysis, but once developed, anything that doesn't contribute to the construction of that metaphoric fort probably has no place in the process. It is important, before we leave this topic, to distinguish the difference between flexibility and common purpose. If the common purpose is the overarching goal, flexibility is essential to an ability to adjust courses as new information is available. Just as each component of the fort needs to be considered for whether or not it contributes to the successful structure, so must each action in the course of a project considered.

And one last note on this: Don't be afraid to be the kid in the back of the minivan who asks, "Why are we doing this again?" The kid who drives the parent crazy can be the person who keeps the enterprise on track.

Civility and Manners

Yes, we're going there. To a certain extent, this is a subset of respect discussed previously. However, whereas respect is largely a mindset, behavior is how that respect—or the lack thereof—gets expressed. To say it another way, you may say you respect someone, but if you treat them badly or rudely, that's difficult to believe. And though this might seem like it has no place in business, it certainly does.

When people do or say heartless or rude things in business, they often excuse it by saying, "It's not personal." That may be true to a certain extent. It's possible for one company to take over another without any personal animosity, even if it's a hostile takeover. It's possible to realize that one has to cut a workforce by X percent without feeling as though you're attacking individuals. Those are clearly business decisions with no human dynamics involved.

But in a group, in an office, in day-to-day interactions, the "it's just business" defense doesn't fly because you are dealing person to person. And people have feelings and responses and so forth, so any interpersonal interaction, no matter how rational the subject matter is, by its very definition is personal.

When I was first starting out in business, rudeness and vulgarity were much more commonplace than they are now. It was distasteful but accepted. It was a little more advanced than the "Mad Men" era, but not so much. I worked in one office where people were routinely subjected to yelling, personal attacks, and statements like "You're an idiot," or worse. When I became a manager, I had a boss who on my performance reviews consistently told me I wasn't "mean enough" to my direct reports, who he believed would be more productive if they lived in fear that they were going to lose their jobs. It wasn't in my nature to be that way, and my people all thrived—many of whom I'm still close to—and I always heard my grandmother in my ear saying, "You catch more flies with honey than with vinegar."

Fortunately in the ensuing decades, the culture has changed, and abusive behavior is no longer accepted or permitted in business, but that's not to say the problem has disappeared entirely, and we still observe and hear about uncivil behavior in businesses.

When I've confronted managers about why they were rude to an employee, I usually get one of three responses. Either they deny being rude and were focused on getting something done urgently, they didn't think about it, or there was no need to treat a person at a lower level well. At the very least, this is shortsighted, and especially in a group setting in a business can backfire. After all, when we invest so much time teaching our children to be polite and expecting them to be so—at least for those who do—why would we not afford the same courtesy to those around us as adults? For many it's a power play or for others, as noted, they don't see the benefit to them.

But let's take a look at this. Think about the people with whom you've worked and the people for whom you've been willing to go the extra mile. Chances are they are people who have treated you well and respectfully. You don't mind going out of your way for someone if they treat you well and show appreciation, because you feel validated and are eager to reciprocate the good treatment.

So, far from being superfluous or unnecessary or a waste of time, civility is a strategic career choice, and a whole lot more pleasant.

My very first job in New York was as the secretary to a C-suite executive. I shared an office with two other secretaries, who worked for the other two executives up there. The guy I worked for was incredibly affable and always very considerate. When he needed something, he'd come to my desk or buzz me to come into his office. He was always very cordial and made sure I understood what was needed. In the 10 months or so I worked for him, we never had a cross word, and I was more than willing to run personal errands and help hide things from his wife (it was the '70s) as a co-conspirator of sorts. It was fun. One of the other execs in our little area used to bark at his secretary without getting up from the desk, threw things on her desk, and generally treated her more as a servant than a co-worker. I don't think my boss spent any more time with me than his colleague did his secretary, but the effect was palpable. I happily stayed late or came in on a weekend, while my colleague never did anything outside of what was required. And why should she have?

No one has ever done a study to confirm it (and I doubt a pure study could be constructed to prove it empirically), but I believe that good manners and civility actually can contribute to the bottom line. Anecdotally we know that when someone is treated badly in a business situation, they look to co-workers to help them get over it. This usually creates bonding around so-and-so being unkind (or more vulgar and picturesque language), which takes a lot of time and energy. A manager who is persistently problematic generally ends up with complaints to HR, which takes a lot of time and energy, and takes away from the productivity of a group. Besides, as I always told my boss who wanted me to be meaner, if people are always afraid that they're going to lose their jobs, keeping their jobs is going to be their first priority, and it's going to color everything they do. I didn't want to participate in creating an atmosphere that is fear-based, because who will take a chance, put themselves out, or take risks? They simply won't do it. Just as the kid who is bullied at school tends to withdraw to escape being tormented, human nature is that we pull away from those things that are threatening. All of this costs money.

Over the years, I've also interviewed and worked with many independent consultants, and all of them have some version of what is often referred to as the "ugly fee." What this means is "This is going to be ugly, so I'm charging a higher fee." This always relates to working with a client who is difficult but also unpleasant to work with. We've all had demanding clients; they come with the territory, but when they're demanding *and* nasty, it's going to cost them. Conversely, for clients who are considerate, like my first boss, I'll go the extra mile. I've routinely not charged for small projects because I want to be supportive, because I like working with the people, and because I know they would do, and have done, the same for me. If you're an independent consultant, I'm betting you have your own version of these scenarios.

And if that's not enough, think of it from the perspective of self-interest. In 2007, I had a project interviewing executives and PR managers about their businesses and corporate cultures. All of them talked about the need for respect at all levels to ensure a healthy and productive work environment. One head of PR for a bank told me that he never hires a senior manager or above without having a meal with him or her. He said he pays attention to everything from table manners to the ability to carry on a social conversation to how he or she treats the servers. All of these are indicators of how someone will be in the personal interactions at a job; it's an insight you can't get in an interview into who someone really is. I've since adopted the practice, and you'd be surprised how revealing it can be.

Who you are and how you are perceived are critically important both for your own career and for your interactions with others. They can be a deciding factor in promotions, getting jobs, and crafting a career. I'm always amazed at how often people forget the "golden rule" of treating others as we would like to be treated, but I've also seen that some of the most successful people in the world treat everyone around them with courtesy and respect because it works—and it makes for a far more pleasant life overall.

As Benjamin Franklin said, "Glass, china, and reputation are easily cracked and never well mended."

Play nice. It pays.

The Challenges in Groups

Effective as they are—and as a way of leveraging talent to achieve tasks—there are several challenges to groups that show up in business all the time with direct relation to the elementary school classroom.

Give everyone a turn. Groups work best when people are actively engaged. If you're running the group, make sure everyone gets a chance to participate and that their participation is valued. If one person is dominating the group, its work, and its decisions, others will tend to withdraw and question why they're involved, and the group won't function effectively as it's intended.

Keep the group focused. Groups always tend to take on a life of their own, and it's easy to get distracted. If you're leading the group, keep them on task.

Reach decisions. One of the most common complaints we hear about group work in companies of all sizes is the inability to get things done. This largely has to do with the personalities and dynamics of the group as well as the need for everyone to be 100 percent on board with every decision. That's never going to happen. For a group to function productively, there has to be a give-and-take among members, to be sure, but a lot of time in groups is wasted trying to make sure everyone is happy, to put it in grade-school terms. Groups that report to a larger organization can build a reporting structure that, for instance, includes recommendations but also acknowledges concerns and reservations. In this case, this is actually more helpful to the people who will make decisions on a group's findings.

What You Can Do
1. Limit the size of groups. Make sure that you have a workable number of people. This is important for such logistical things as scheduling but also for productivity in working sessions. For example, have one person from accounting in the group. It will be that person's job to interact with other members of the accounting department and represent them to the group.

	What You Can Do (continued)
2.	Don't form a group without a clear objective. You may have a specific committee that covers various things over time, but goals should be clearly delineated so the group has a common purpose.
3.	Balance thinking styles within a group. Diversity of thinking styles will provide a foundation for considering more possibilities and courses of action.
4.	Establish a chairperson of the group who is charged with keeping the group on track but who is also able to deal with the inevitable challenges of balancing personalities and keep the group functioning.
5.	Change up groups to keep the thinking and approach to challenges fresh.

Boys and Girls Play Differently

There is a brief window in childhood when girls and boys play similarly—up to about age 4, actually. Before then, their play is virtually indistinguishable. Granted, it's not very elaborate: stacking, sorting, grabbing, pulling. Even classic toys like Fisher-Price's Little People started out as generic pegs with faces. (Before adults got their thinking on them, but that's another story.)

Then at age 4, children begin to gender differentiate, which is a fancy way of saying that they begin to understand that they are boys and girls, and the two are not alike. This is the age at which they start to play "doctor" and are able to understand what's different about their bodies.

Though that's a gross simplification, from that point on, behaviors, interactions, and approaches to the world are dictated in large part by these gender differences. This often comes as a shock to parents who have gotten used to a little girl and then get a little boy, but the difference is wired into us from the get-go, and there's not much we can do about it.

Nor do we grow out of it. In her economical and insightful book, *Sex, Lies & Creativity*, author and life coach Julia Roberts describes the physical and chemical changes that influence behavior for kids and throughout life. She demonstrates how human behavior, perception, and interaction are driven by hormones as much as by sociological influences. Indeed, she demonstrates how the changing chemical makeups of our bodies at different times in our lives are likely to drive behaviors. Understanding this is helpful to the point that it explains how genders differ naturally—thanks to our friends estrogen and testosterone—and that there's not much we can do about it. These gender differences were essential when humans filled more traditionally mammalian roles. In other words, the men went out and hunted, and the women took care of the cave and the kids. In our more enlightened age—with civilization, indoor plumbing, and the threat of being eaten reduced exponentially—it's possible for people to take on roles or functions that might have traditionally been defined by gender. Social evolution is much faster than physical evolution, and no matter how intellectually enlightened we are, we still have that makeup more suited to the prehistoric hunter-gatherer than the contemporary office worker. In other words, modern social structures put some demands on both men and women that don't come naturally to us as mammals. So, we have to work on it.

But bringing it back to play for a moment, when all the biology is taken away, boys and girls really fall into two distinct camps: Boys like power and conflict. Girls like nurturing and cooperation. In the late 1990s, we created a test where we put boys with traditional girls' toys and girls with traditional boys' toys. The kids were all of kindergarten age—5 or 6. We left them alone to see what they would do. Within a relatively short time, after the kids went through the stage of becoming comfortable with the other children in the room, we had boys whacking each other with dolls and using them as weapons and girls creating a family of vehicles that they had given characters and a social hierarchy to. This is how they interacted without adult supervision or guidance. Although we believe that this gender difference is the product of physical and biological patterning rather than social patterning (nature rather than nurture, in other words), it really doesn't matter. *The boys and girls played differently.* When at the end of the play session, the boys and girls were brought together. Each group gravitated to the toys that were more consistent with their traditional gender roles and continued playing in the same way among their own gender. (At this age, co-play is shared space rather than interaction.)

You probably don't need reams of research to convince you that boys and girls remain just as different as they get older. Boys love grossout humor. Girls love pretty collectibles. Boys like *The Three Stooges.* Girls don't. Men, as they move into their professional years, tend to be aggressive, looking for individual achievement and recognition. Women tend to like to create strong teams. Men are more likely to be dictatorial in their decision-making and management style, whereas women tend to want to build consensus. Before you get mad at me, remember we're talking in general terms, and we're not trying to call out any individuals. But think about times when you were in conflict with a member of the opposite sex, and ask yourself if gender chemistry had anything to do with it. It's a worthwhile exercise because it opens you open to being more tolerant and understanding, and that's a critical area for forming the interpersonal relationships that are critical to a successful working environment. If you can't think of any of the top of your head, turn on the TV. From *Dr. Phil* to sitcoms to cartoons, differences in behavior or thinking that can be traced to gender are everywhere.

Real people exist along a spectrum of these gender differences. Age, socialization, education level, personality, and experience can all affect how the biological imperatives of gender are expressed in individuals, but they are always going to be there. Roberts shows how gay men and lesbians, for example, may share more of the brain chemistry of the opposite gender. She adds that as men age and their testosterone levels decrease, they are less likely to be aggressive and competitive, particularly in their 50s, what Roberts calls a "harvest mind." At the same time, women at that age who are past childbearing are looking for new challenges and new ways to be relevant, what she calls "beginners' mind." The point Roberts is making is that these differences are part of who we are and we have to learn to live with them. That's certainly part of relationships, but it's also true in business.

Sadly, acknowledging these differences often becomes forbidden and helps drive conflict, whereas acceptance might facilitate understanding. Can you imagine in a contemporary office suggesting "She approached the problem that way because she's a woman"? A man who said that would instantly be branded a sexist and vilified. But the fact of the matter is, given the situation, she might have approached a problem in a certain way because that's how her brain is wired.

So, if you're a man and you think that, you probably don't want to say that out loud because you're bound to be misunderstood. But as a manager or a co-worker, understanding how the people you work with are going to approach any given problem based on gender can be a real advantage.

Again, we're going to generalize, but men tend to want to take action and move things along, and everyone else can follow or get out of the way. They also believe that they can wing it or power through a situation. We see this constantly when men and women have to work together on a proposal, for example. The women on the team want to rehearse and plan every aspect of it, whereas the men are content with a more general knowledge of where it's going.

Women, on the other hand, are more likely to seek consensus of all involved and gather as much information as possible before making a decision. We've seen it too many times to doubt that this dynamic is very often at play in work situations. And you probably have as well, but you may not have thought about it as naturally occurring because of gender and biology. More likely, whichever side of the issue you were on, you were probably annoyed with the other person and didn't understand why they wanted to do something in a way that surely wasn't going to work. What this sometimes leads to are pitched battles, non-productive conflict, and politics.

A side note on politics: Men and women play that game differently as well. We're going to go back to our prehistoric roots again. Men are likely to be aggressive and dominant, using power to get what they want. Women, on the other hand, are more likely to be quietly manipulative and work behind the scenes to get what they want. What always boggles my mind is that no one wants to talk about it, even when it happens right in front of them, and they refuse to acknowledge that gender differences might have anything to do with it. This is, not to put too fine a point on it, idiotic. In stressful situations, people are always going to revert to their inherent natures. Our current cultural environment, however, says we're not supposed to talk about it in that way. We'll get to why in a moment, but I often want to say to people, "You see those nature shows on TV? We're exactly like that." The challenge, of course, is that our natural instincts and inclinations developed when physical survival was a daily question, and those are still in us. Don't kid yourself.

Recently, the marketing department of a major company we consulted to had a terrific shakeup, and the futures of all but a few of the employees and senior managers were in question. You might as well have said, "Let the games begin!" because that's what happened. And it fell out along gender lines as well. The men were largely aggressive in promoting themselves and their achievements as being superior to the others in the department. The women, on the other hand, played a different game, trying to insinuate themselves with the senior managers—male or female—based on building or reinforcing relationships. When the axes finally fell, it was impossible to tell what the real reasons were for the firings, because all the announcements were made in completely neutral terms, as befits a publicly traded company that wants to avoid employment suits at all costs. That is, obviously, the only way to go with something like that. Still, human dynamics are always at play. By the way, more women were left than men.

Before we go on, I do want to throw in a brief aside about sexism. Sexism exists, and we've seen it hurt companies, departments, and individuals. It's a terrible mind-set that can create a horrible and hostile working environment for all involved, and it's something that needs to be addressed at the highest levels of a company. That extends to jokes, comments, and generally disrespectful comments or attitudes. These have no place in a work environment. But sexism is not the subject here. Rather, what we're talking about is pretty much the opposite of sexism; it is an appreciation of the inevitable differences between the genders and an invitation to admit that these differences exist, embrace them, and see how they can be leveraged to make a better working environment and greater success for all involved.

The problem is that the topic of gender has become so loaded in today's workplace, however, that *any* mention of it is presumed to be negative. I've had senior executives at publicly traded companies flat out refuse to discuss this with me as it relates to play and business, even privately. I get it, and I sympathize, but at the same time, we avoid these issues at our peril. So, perhaps we can all think about it quietly. I'm only half kidding.

But what can you do? Well, again we can take the hint from children. Kids don't behave well to adult standards naturally. They have to be socialized. One of the things they have to be socialized into is respect. It has to be taught and modeled so they can practice it and make it part of their behavior in the world. Most parents try to teach children to appreciate differences in one another and accept those. The same goes for adults.

Michele Litzky, who for the past 20 years or so has run Litzky Public Relations (LPR), says that respect is the most important element of creating a positive working environment. The majority of the LPR employees are women, and when I raised the issue of gender with her, she said that it didn't figure in her hiring decisions. Instead, she said, "We're in a business that seems to naturally attract more women, but what we're looking for are people who want to grow, learn, and succeed." However, gender does figure in her understanding of the dynamics with clients.

She says, "We had one client who always liked to kiss all the women, and that made them somewhat uncomfortable. But then we realized, he's an older guy, and this is the way he does something. You can't really call it sexual harassment, though I suppose someone could. But you also can't be running to a lawyer every five minutes, either, when you've got a business to run." Still, Litzky had to set boundaries as gently as she could and ultimately resigned the client.

Litzky acknowledges that gender may determine how some of the people she works with act, or how they approach life and work, and she stresses that that is only one element of a working relationship. She says that she tries to understand, respect, and appreciate people as individuals and accept them as they are, but she is also neither a pushover or afraid of confrontation. Interestingly enough, however, she only confronts when pushed to it, and then almost exclusively to protect her business or her employees, which would often be considered a more female trait. She also has had the advantage of running her own show for more than two decades. Yet her emphasis on respect above all is clearly one contributor to her success. Most of her employees have been with her for the long term, as have her clients.

One of the reasons that public relations tends to attract more women is that very often the nature of the work is about teamwork, process, and getting consensus. In the case of crisis PR, it's also about defusing aggression. If these are more female traits, so be it. There's nothing sexist about appreciating people's native or inherent skills and using them to advantage. That's a kind of professional Darwinism. There are many men who are experts in PR as well, and the field was largely established in the early 1900s by Edward Louis Bernays and others, but still various estimates places the percentage of women to men in the field at anywhere from 63 to 85 percent.

In today's world, the single-gender work environment is virtually non-existent. There are always exceptions, like the office portrayed in the movie *The Wolf of Wall Street*, which was more mythic than mainstream and pandered to a romantic (largely male) fantasy of the never-ending frat party with lots and lots of money. (They seldom make movies about your average publishing company, say.) So the genders inevitably have to mix, and that's a good thing, as the assets of both can be leveraged more effectively. Mars and Venus, to use the nearly exhausted pop psychology phrase, can't merely move in the same orbit; they need to align.

And that's really where the opportunity lies. The complementary nature of these inherent gender differences is a remarkable asset, and one that's relatively new in the history of work. For the savvy worker or manager, knowing how to use and balance these dynamics without bias is an essential skill.

We like to remind people of what it was like when they played "doctor" as kids—and we've yet to find a kid who didn't. It was curiosity and exploration without judgment, discovering, appreciating, and being amazed by the similarities and the obvious differences and an introduction into the nature of being human.

What You Can Do

1.	Take some time to think about your gender identity and where you fit on the spectrum from male to female. Think about how your actions may be guided by your hormonal makeup, no matter what age you are.
2.	Review your working relationships—past and present—with members of the opposite sex, and consider how and when gender differences may have influenced those relationships.
3.	Think about one situation that didn't go well for you and analyze how it turned out as it did, paying particular attention to the turning point and what you did. What might you have done differently if you had adapted some traits of the opposite gender? (Just because you're built one way, that doesn't mean you can't consciously appropriate other behaviors. After all, human beings are marvelously adaptive.)
4.	Take a look at your closest non-romantic relationship with a member of the opposite gender. What works about it? What are the traits of that person you admire? Are they gender related? Where are you similar?
5.	Accept yourself for who you are, knowing that although you may not be responsible for your first thoughts and impulses, you are responsible for your actions. You've got to work with what you've got, and getting to know that is critical. Once you get that down, start to make room for others to be as they are. You'll find this opens up new levels of communicating that can be highly effective.

Play Is Assessing Information, Taking Risks, and Taking Action

Recently, a great deal of focus in certain sectors of the toy industry has been placed on the need to get preschoolers active as a way of encouraging health and preventing childhood obesity. That's all very well and good; no one wants to see children being unhealthy. But what boggles the mind is that anyone who has spent any time with a healthy preschooler knows that getting him or her active isn't the problem. Getting a kid to sit down and be still is more difficult. For our purposes, however, we want to talk about play as an active process of discovery and information-processing. In the adult world, and particularly in business, this shows up as ongoing choices, experimentation, feedback, and new choices based on the feedback. This is a radical simplification of Piaget's theories of child development and constructivist theory, and I encourage you to delve into that if you're interested, but for our purposes, it can be boiled down to the bromide that experience is the most effective teacher, and as children begin to accumulate experiences and information, and as their brains and personalities become more developed, they learn to make more sophisticated choices.

Play is an active process, and for children engaged in play, action is a constant. Whether they are building something with LEGOs, running around the backyard, or engaged in solving problems, they are constantly acquiring more information and experience. In the world of kids, the advent of video games and other sedentary activities as well as the decline of the unstructured neighborhood play most Baby Boomers recall has meant that many kids may be less physically active today than they were a generation ago. Nonetheless, we don't want to confuse physical action with active imagination and decision-making, which is what's always going on whether it's expressed physically or mentally.

Play is also very much about embracing risk and uncertainty, and taking an action even when the outcome is not guaranteed. In fact, acting without a known outcome is the very essence of play, and the best teacher there is. Trying something you haven't done before begins to build a frame of reference for that activity and a wealth of experience that provides you with the subconscious analytical tools (we'll talk about "intuition" in a bit) that are essential to making good decisions.

In the neighborhood where I grew up, garage roofs were fairly close together—no more than about 3 feet apart. One of the rites of passage in our group of friends was being able to jump from one roof to the other. This is a big deal when you're 7 or 8, and a bit scary, but once accomplished, it was a huge badge of honor. I can't recall any kid ever falling, by the way, though we got plenty banged up riding bikes, climbing trees, and doing other activities. Objectively speaking, danger in the roof jump was much greater in our minds than in reality; we were all capable of jumping 3 feet. However, we made the risk and the stakes enormous in our minds, and ultimately overcoming those laid the foundation for taking greater risks.

I never rode a skateboard when I was a kid; it was one of the few things that my parents forbade. However, a few years ago, I was required to learn how to ride one for a TV thing I was doing. It was not a skill easily acquired by this middle-aged man, but I figured I could do it, and I did. I also had the opportunity, for another TV thing, to go off the ski jump training platform in Park City, Utah. This is a long slide—in skis and a wet suit—down an Astroturf-covered ski jump. At the end of the platform, you lift off, jump, and land in a swimming pool, skis and all. I looked ridiculous and did something with an hour's training that serious ski jumpers don't do for weeks. But we got the shot.

I bring these up because they are really about the essence of active play: the ongoing assessment of risk juxtaposed against projected or desired result. When I give presentations and I'm asked how I got to do the work I do, after I tell them I made it up (the essence of imaginary play), I always say that there is one sentence that has guided my career: "Sure, I'll try that." This is not some cavalier statement; it is based on an ability to assess risk based on my experience and assessment of my capabilities. Assured by the Olympic coaches that even a mediocre skier, which I most certainly am, could get off the jump without injury and get the shot we needed, I decided to go for it. And speaking of skiing, one of the other great lessons I learned about business happened on a ski slope. I was an adult when I finally achieved my wish of learning to ski, but it was terrifying. I had a great young instructor, however, who told me that I'd never get anywhere if I didn't point my skis down the hill. It was scary and felt like a risk, and I certainly had my spills, but eventually I learned to ski. A close friend of mine who has started and sold several businesses in different industries is fond of paraphrasing famous salesman Zig Ziglar, saying, "Anything worth doing is worth doing poorly until you can do it better."

Risk is also one of the defining elements of innovation. In business, risk is often defined as venturing into the unknown or something that hasn't been tried before, and given the investment in being successful, it becomes fraught with all kinds of issues related to return on investment and trying to predict outcomes, sometimes with relatively little information. The result of risk is profit or loss, and that can be scary.

In terms of play, however, the result of risk is always learning, and risk brings with it the absolute guarantee of some level of failure. Without failure, however, there can be no progress. If you're going to be innovative, there's no way to do it without failure. If you already knew how to do something, then it wouldn't be new, right? If you want to learn to play the piano, you can't skip the stage where you sound just dreadful as you play. There's no way around it. The risk of sitting down to play and clearing the room as you're beginning is offset by the vision of being able to play down the road. But you have to take the risk and take the action in order to get there. The question becomes: How much risk can you handle to make progress? It's an important question to ask because, just as it defines a company, it can also define your career.

Most leading companies fit somewhere toward the center of the high-risk/low-risk continuum. Most people do, too. If you've sat with a financial advisor, they're probably done a risk-assessment profile with you to see how conservative or aggressive they can or should be with your portfolio. For the most part, people tend to fall around the middle of the continuum, and so do companies, though that can vary and contributes to the cyclical nature of business.

Company dynamics can be very much like human dynamics in that when there are threats of any nature and people feel vulnerable, they tend to turn inward, whereas in good times when people are feeling secure, they tend to be outward-focused and looking for new opportunities for expansion. Also, like people, there are risks in going to extremes. Too much inward focus and being careful, and the company will stagnate. Too much risk, and the basic stability of the company is potentially jeopardized.

You can think of it in terms of genetics, and it's actually quite interesting to do so. A species that's mutating with every generation isn't going to survive any more than one that doesn't evolve at all—or quickly enough—to meet changing conditions. In biology, random mutations are a kind of cellular risk that either help the species adapt to a dynamic world and are passed on to next generations, or disappear. Same thing with companies, with the exception that the risks (or, for the sake of our metaphor, the mutations) are hopefully more strategic than random.

Innovation and Creativity

Taken in this way, innovation and creativity are essential to the evolution of a company and its continued progress over time. Companies and managers that foster creativity and innovation are those that are able to create a culture in which risk and failure are actually encouraged. They create an environment that embraces risk as a learning and discovery process. Like evolution, it's a long-term effort, however, and as we'll see in a bit, faces significant headwind, especially in the current market because it is time-consuming and expensive. This can be especially challenging for public companies that need to show results more quickly than the process might allow to not be punished by Wall Street. (The exceptions to this are companies like Amazon that manage to maintain high stock prices even when profits wouldn't seem to justify them. See Chapter 2 for more on this phenomenon.)

As described, creative play is one of the most active things children do, engaging them mentally, physically, and often, emotionally. The same holds true in companies. Investing in creativity goes to the very essence of play in that something is made up in the imagination and then brought into reality. There are tons of books on creativity, developing your creativity, and so forth. We take a very simple, and hopefully childlike, point of view on this. It's most analogous to taking a whole box of LEGOs, for instance, dumping it out on the floor, and saying, "Well, now what can we make with this that's new?" In this case, we'll let the LEGO pieces represent everything you know about your business, all its various parts and pieces, and then you just dive in and play. I know this probably sounds too simple, but you just have to take everything you know and let it jostle around, and allow yourself to have a steady stream of ideas of the various different ways you could put these pieces together and whether you need new pieces, and allow your new structure to take shape in your imagination and see where it takes you. You don't need fancy seminars. Really, you need only what that kid with the LEGOs has: clarity of vision and confidence.

These are essential because they'll guide the active, creative process and keep you on track. A significant part of the process in business, however, is being able to distinguish a good idea from a bad one. For our purposes, we'll define a good idea as one that could be developed into a viable product or practice and a bad one as one that can't.

The stark reality is that many of the ideas you'll come up with—some people estimate 50 percent or more—aren't going to be viable and should be dropped cold. The process of play is sorting through all those ideas to find the one that you think might be worth investing your time, just as a child goes through a toy store looking at products on the shelf, trying to decide where to invest his or her allowance. I know that probably sounds a bit trite, but it really is the case, and you can't shortchange the process.

So how do you decide what to move forward with? Well, that's where the "gut" comes in, at least partially. Yes, you're going to do all your due diligence and research and statistical analysis, but at the end of the day, people and companies rely a great deal more on their gut—or intuition—than they do on statistics, and that's not necessarily a bad thing. For instance, if you are considering buying an expensive watch or something else you'd like to have but isn't essential for survival, you're going to marshal all the data to support that decision. Conversely, if you decide not to purchase it, your rationales will all support that decision. This is human nature because we want to feel good about the decisions we make. The way we think of it is that you can collect all the data in the world and you can use it to inform your choice and to justify the choice you make, but that moment of choice is something else altogether. One of my very first mentors put it this way, with respect to personal relationships: "You can give someone all the support and information you can up to the point where they have to make a decision. And, if you can, you support them after they make the decision. But you can't make that decision for them." In my experience and in talking with many people about the choices they've made, this holds true. (Even when a decision is reached by committee, each individual member has to make a choice individually.)

Making those choices can be one of the most exciting things that you do because that moment is the essence of creativity. It's when you become that kid and say, "Let's make something." We're not the only species that makes things, by the way. Birds make nests, bees make hives, and so forth, but they do that instinctively and automatically. The *choice* to create something from nothing, however, is distinctly human and unique compared to any other species on the planet, and it's part of what makes living an adventure.

The Power of the "Gut," or Intuition

As mentioned, before we go on, I want to take a moment to talk about intuition and its role in the creative process. When I talk to executives who have been successful with projects or businesses, sooner or later the issue of intuition comes up. When I asked the CEO of a major consumer products company why his line in 2014 was so much better than his line in 2013, he said that they had systematically gone through the company and put the best product people in charge, without respect to seniority or longevity with the company. When pressed as to how he and his team knew that these were the best product people, he claimed that a significant component of the decisions was intuitive. Intuition is often hailed as being mystical, a "sixth sense," something that only rare people in business possess. This may make good headlines and feature stories, but largely it's hogwash. Intuition is nothing more than the fearless, and subconscious, application of accumulated knowledge to an immediate problem. It does not spring mystically from the ether. It is not "received wisdom" or anything even remotely supernatural. It is a function of experience and brain chemistry. It only becomes mystical when someone tells you they know something, but they can't tell you how they know it—and they're right.

Given this example, the senior executives had plenty of information about how individual executives worked, how the products they developed performed, and their knowledge of the market and its opportunities. This all gets filed in the brain under experiences with that individual to be drawn upon when interacting with that individual. Rather than trace each bit of knowledge back to its source, they trust themselves and their experience to be able to know what's right in a given situation. Although it's very powerful and a great asset, there's nothing mysterious about it. My brother, who was always a huge baseball fan, was always able to watch a game on TV and predict what the next play would be. He was amazingly accurate. I certainly couldn't do that. I can, however, look at a toy line in development and tell you which products have a better chance of success, and more often than not, I'm right. This is not because angels are whispering in my ears; it's because I have more than 30 years' experience working hands-on with toys, watching the market, seeing what does well, and studying children, observing their relationship to the culture, and staying up on larger trends in consumer culture, as well. All that information has been packed away over the years. I'm not a neuroscientist, so I don't know how it works, but I do know that when presented with a new product or concept the mind makes a huge amount of associations almost instantaneously. An ability to access and process a lot of information from your experience is an asset, but it's neither mystical nor that unusual, as long as you're willing to trust your own experience and mental process. You can think of it this way: You're a walking, talking, breathing algorithm. That may make it a little easier to accept for those of you who are driven by data. I'm slightly kidding, of course. The downside of thinking of intuition or the gut as something mystical means that normal, rational people aren't going to trust it, or trust themselves.

And don't get me wrong: Just as a doctor would use every technique possible to diagnose a patient, your gut or intuition should only be one tool you use, because it can backfire as well. As Ronald Reagan said, "Trust but verify." As with the disastrous toy that came to the president of that small toy company in a dream and bombed, despite his gut feeling that little girls everywhere would love it, your intuition is only as good as the data that it's pulling from—like an algorithm, which is only as good as the variables it considers.

One example of this I often use when I talk about the intuition and algorithms is one that you probably experience every day. Let's say you're looking to buy a lamp and you shop online. For the next period of time, every time you go to a site that rents out space to search engine advertising, you're going to see ads for lamps. That makes sense, unless you bought a lamp on the first day you were looking. Then all those ads are meaningless to you, and you ignore them. The algorithm, however, doesn't know that you bought a lamp, so it can't suggest a rug based on your lamp purchase. Because the algorithm can't collect that information, for many sensible reasons, it is therefore limited.

The human mind, however, is not limited. Watch kids play, particularly when they're engaged in open-ended, narrative play as with action figures and dolls. They are drawing on all kinds of information that they've stored and filtered it through the narrative, and—boom—they've got a sometimes incredibly rich story going on. Another way of looking at it is if you've ever had the experience of a child saying something that you think of as "out of the blue." You scratch your head or tell your friends, "I don't know how she came up with that." But really it's very simple: The child's mind is constantly making connections and identifying relationships, which are unseen by you and which would not occur to you. That's the wonder of the human brain. Why we don't trust it more in the context of other data and research always boggles my mind. We tend to dismiss people with a "You just think that" or, "Yes, but that's just an opinion." Consider the source. I'll gladly take the *opinion* about my gallbladder from someone who's been practicing medicine for the 30 years, for example.

The great news about developing intuition or gut is that it's actually easily done, if you're willing to make the investment of time and study. You do not have to go to an ashram and learn to meditate, which to me only sounds attractive conceptually, so you are in an open space where you can hear the music of the spheres or some such tripe. Rather, developing intuition is about gathering as much information and input as you can in all kinds of forms, and letting your mind do its job. This, by the way, is why the liberal arts are so essential for developing skills that are necessary for business because they allow you to develop, and ultimately draw on, proficiency in all different kinds of disciplines. Indeed, some of the savviest and most successful businesspeople I know did their undergraduate work in the liberal or even fine arts.

At this writing, there are many efforts in the United States to focus primary and secondary education more on skills needed to perform in the current job market. I certainly applaud efforts to teach kids coding, which is one of these efforts, but not because it's a finite skill. Coding combines both divergent (What all could we do?) and convergent (Here's what we'll actually do.) thinking. The flaw with this thinking, however, is that preparing kids for the current job market doesn't prepare them to adapt when the market changes. Learning Latin, for example, is not a waste of time, though it's certainly not something used every day. Learning Latin helps kids learn how to learn—to analyze and break something down into its component parts and then put it back together again. When looked at closely in this light, however, the pedagogical benefit of learning coding is very similar to learning Latin. This skill, in turn, becomes part of the knowledge base that can be drawn on in other situations.

You're not going to dust off Cicero, I know, and you probably won't sign up for a coding class. But if you want to build your gut or intuitive sense, feed it with as much diverse information as you can. Go to movies and plays. Watch sports. Immerse yourself in the wonderful diversity of culture, and if you can, see it with a child's eyes when he or she looks at everything as new. And if you're entering an industry you haven't worked in before, educate yourself about its history, successes, and failures. Then listen and observe and give your amazing brain the time it needs to make the connections, which, fortunately, isn't that long. And I don't want to hear that you're too old or that if you'd learned Mandarin when you were 2, it would have been possible. I know plenty of people in their 50s and even 60s who have learned new languages, entered new industries, or started businesses. Given the chance, you'll be amazed at how much your gut or instinct can grow, and you may even have more to say at cocktail parties.

Speaking Of: Let's Talk About Genius

At some point, every parent thinks little Num-Num is a "genius" and proudly shouts that from the rooftop—or more likely Facebook, which is the contemporary version of that.

And what has the child done to receive such an accolade? Well, probably he or she has done something the parent didn't think he or she could at that age. Where we see this often these days is in the statement, "My 1-year-old can work the iPad!" Of course the child can. By that age they have the physical coordination to touch the pad and the understanding that if they touch an icon, something will happen. Parents, and especially grandparents, think this is "genius" because the iPad didn't exist when they were small, so it's new to them. But it's not to the baby. They have seen it on a parent's lap since day one. Of course they're going to be curious.

I mention this because genius, like intuition, is often misunderstood in today's world, and certainly in the business world. Calling someone a genius is, on one level, recognizing someone who is extraordinary, but it's often used as a means of denigrating oneself. I have talked to a lot of people in jobs or in career transition who talk about so-and-so being a genius. Of course, there are many high-profile people who are regularly considered to be geniuses: Steve Jobs, who revolutionized computing, telephony, and music purchasing; Alan Turing, the father of the algorithm and computing science; Jill Barad, who rescued the Barbie brand and drove its exponential growth—and the list goes on and on.

While taking nothing away from any of these people, of whom I and millions of others stand in awe, it may be useful to look at the source of their genius. It was as simple as this: It's seeing something clearly where others don't. It's the ability to see a problem or an opportunity from a different perspective. Think of all the cases where there has been an insoluble problem, and someone comes along and comes up with a solution, after which people think it's obvious. And that solution really comes from a simple statement, such as "Well, what if we think about it this way?"

Let's talk about Barad and Barbie for a moment. In the early 1980s, the world was changing, and Barbie was facing all kinds of new challenges from a variety of different toys, yes, but also a changing zeitgeist related to kids of Barbie age, their social world, and their interaction with peers. Barbie play had always been aspirational, as kids projected themselves into the magical world of being a teenager (As seen from a 6-year-old's perspective; we try not to disappoint them at that age.). Barad re-conceived the relationship between girls and their Barbie dolls in light of how girls were interacting in the culture. The result was that Barbie was not some aspirational icon but rather a peer. Virtually anyone who was a child in 1985 remembers the commercial that did it: "We girls can do anything. Right, Barbie?" What made it work as advertising, however, was not the abstract statement of girl empowerment; it was the "Right, Barbie?" that inextricably tied Barbie to the statement and established her as a peer to the girls who wanted to feel that level of power. Barbie became a focus and a totem onto which girls wanted to project their sense of self as fun and capable—the best possible advertising strategy. Sales skyrocketed, and Barad was hailed as a genius—which she was, especially as we're defining it. But it's important to note that it was the willingness to see a legacy brand in a new way that completely revitalized it. It's also important to note that Barad didn't do this in a vacuum. She had lots of research and testing to draw on, but it was her leadership, vision, and confidence that propelled the brand forward.

Genius is everywhere in kids. In fact, it's the very essence of play. But genius is fragile, and it's very easily socialized out of kids. A kid who thinks of things in a different way may not fit in easily to a group.

Adults correct kids who play with a toy in a way other than what was intended. What is free, associative, and open-ended play in kids can be perceived as threatening to parents.

This is the underlying theme of *The LEGO Movie*, and it really is a must-watch as a way of understanding the power and benefits of play and as a design for living and business. The essential conflict is between a child whose free-flowing imagination admits a full range of possibilities and an order-obsessed adult who wants everything to conform to a rigid design that admits no variation and is literally stuck in place. It's a wonderful twist by the screenwriters that the villain who wants everything set and unchanging is named Lord Business.

In any business, the potential for genius really is everywhere. All it takes is a willingness to look at things from a different perspective. As we continue to say about play, the imaginative process is one of the most cost-effective practices you can engage in. Welcome new perspectives and new ideas because whether you take them or not, they only make you better.

One other thing about geniuses: They don't tend to think of themselves in that way. Their insights and ideas come out of their knowledge, how they see the world, and how they approach a challenge. The fact is they simply can't do it another way. Fostering new ways of thinking is one of the best things you can do for your business. In other words, allow people to play and see what happens.

As with Lord Business, the sense of security and stability may, in fact, be an illusion. Had Barad insisted that Barbie not evolve, it probably would have died out, and if one looks at Barbie's success over the years, even with occasional dips in sales, the history of that brand is that it has consistently been revived by new ways of thinking about it in the context of a changing world.

Let other people decide whether or not you're a genius; you just keep playing. That's the way to move forward.

Stalled: The Pervasive Challenge of Risk Aversion

Just as we said that all you need to be creative is clarity of vision and confidence, the opposite of that is fear and risk aversion. In 2015, risk aversion is a challenge faced by companies at all levels of the economy. It's understandable. It's human, and it's toxic.

Not surprisingly, risk aversion, also known as fear, is the greatest inhibitor in kids' play as well. In play, at least, we see many kids whose fear of not being successful stops them from trying. We see this in everything from piano lessons to sports to schoolwork. Encouraging kids to take risks—within reason, of course—is critical to their development both in terms of mastery of any given task and self-confidence. The time to learn this is when kids are young and relatively protected from the consequences of their risks as they learn about themselves and their capabilities. Encouraging them to take risks, within reason, and not worry about failing sets the stage for a more fearless future. Unfortunately, we live in a culture today, in the United States at least, where every decision or action a child takes is given tremendous, and largely unwarranted, importance. Kids are guided to the right activities for their school transcripts, for example, by parents who are well-meaning and believe that they're helping their kids, but who, in fact, are putting so much emphasis on the results that the child is removed from the process. Kids are being put on a track that admits for very little variation.

In 2012, we followed three 11th graders through the college application process because we had been hearing from parents how stressful it was for the kids and the families. This was not any kind of formal study. Rather, we checked in with the young people and their parents at different times of the year. What we found over the course of the year was that virtually everything these young people did was with an eye to how it would affect the college admissions process—from what activities to participate in to sports to trying to determine what community service projects would look best on a transcript. Moreover, any wrong choice—any falling short—was freighted with the fear of not being accepted in college. The pressure on these kids was very high, and no wonder it was stressful. Though our final observations were not scientific, based on subsequent interviews with college-bound students, we concluded they were representative and indicative. The pressure on these young people to achieve college admissions made them risk-averse in that they were unwilling to try anything that could derail their chances, at least for two of them. The most unfortunate part was that they felt the pressure to meet a standard and an outcome over which they ultimately had very little control, and in the process of trying to meet that goal strove to fit into a specific mold rather than discover who they were as individuals. One young woman seemed to feel the pressure less. Partly because she had the confidence to follow her own interests and search for colleges, whether Ivy League or not, that complemented her interests and partly because her parents encouraged her be her own person, she seemed to keep the whole process in perspective. She got into the school she ultimately wanted to get into after she did her own research, by the way, and at this writing is thriving in her sophomore year.

I bring this up because it illustrates a larger issue: From where we sit, risk aversion is becoming a serious problem in our culture, as well as in business. We are teaching it an early age and putting focus on avoiding risk, rather than assessing risk in any situation and plotting a course of action that takes the risk into account. The kid who is afraid that any false move might jeopardize his chances at getting into a good college becomes the kid afraid of not getting into the right graduate school and so forth. Now, you're always going to see the kid who makes the killer app, who leaves college to create a startup and so forth, but the reason those stories make the news is because they are unusual. Play is a process of sequential discovery, and new action. If we teach kids to play in this way, rather than try to hit a specific target, falling short and, yes, failing, should not be devastating; it should be instructive. My grandmother liked to say, "When the Lord closes a door, he opens a window." I tend to prefer to think like Indiana Jones who, whenever it looked like it was disaster, always seemed to find a way out. That's pure play in action.

It's also the basis for creative entrepreneurship. Talk to virtually any entrepreneur, and he or she will tell you that they made "every possible mistake" getting to where they are. Well, every mistake, perhaps, except one: They never gave up.

In business, risks have more direct consequences, expressed as revenue, career, and so on, but at a certain point, just like pointing one's skis down the hill, you have to take action if you're going to get anything done.

I interviewed a recent graduate of the Harvard Business School about the climate of risk aversion she sees around her as she's trying to establish a startup in business-to-business merchandising. "MBAs make PowerPoints," she said. "That's what we do. We make PowerPoints about the PowerPoints we're going to make because we're all so risk-averse. We want to build models, and spin out scenarios. That's what we're trained to do." These exercises are about trying to know the unknowable, as we've discussed earlier, and really the whole process is about trying to control that which you really can't control—outcomes of choices and actions. (Cue the nuns singing "How Do You Solve a Problem Like Maria?" here. It's a nice little reality check that illustrates how much of life is really outside our control.) What you can do is make the choice, take the action, and then respond, as we've said previously. Actually, if you think about it, Maria Von Trapp—in life and in the movies—was the antithesis of risk aversion. She responded to each new event as it came up and took action. (You don't have time to do a PowerPoint if you have to get out of Austria before they close the borders.)

All kidding about *The Sound of Music* aside, however, like anything in life, risk aversion can be smart. The kid who wasn't ready to jump between the garage roofs protected himself from injury, for example. The business that doesn't rush headlong into a new project without a full-scale analysis protects itself from a costly mistake. No person in their right mind is going to take a risk when the preponderance of available evidence suggests that the chances of failure are greater than the chances of success.

At a certain point, though, if risk aversion leads to inaction, the results can be as damaging as a failure because of a missed opportunity—depending on how you look at it.

A mid-sized toy company was dealing with a major retailer, selling them an item that was slowly building sales momentum. Ultimately, it took off and in the last few months of the year, all retailers stocking that item were having a hard time keeping it in stock. The toy company was working feverishly and shipping pretty much round the clock to keep up with demand, which—thanks to some good marketing and a serendipitous and newfound popularity for this type of product—was steadily growing. As always happens in this type of situation, the trick is to be able to keep pace with demand but not over-ship so as to flood the market and kill it. (This happens all the time in the toy industry.) Notwithstanding, every retailer with the exception of one major was taking every piece of merchandise they could get, especially as it became obvious that even with ramping up production to full capacity the toy company would not be able to meet all the demand for product. The sales reps and executives from the company were trying to convince the retailer to take additional product, particularly as his customers were asking for it. However, the buyer refused, saying that they had met their quota for the season and weren't going to take any more product.

This made no sense to the toy company, and ostensibly makes no sense to anyone on the surface, because we would naturally assume that, with high demand, the opportunity for increased revenue is obvious and in this case virtually guaranteed—that is, until you dig a little deeper and understand what's truly at stake, which in this case is not increased sales or revenue for the company but the buyer's performance and bonus.

The way it works is this: A buyer makes a commitment to purchase a certain quantity of product for his department. If that product sells through and achieves its revenue target, the buyer is a hero and receives a bonus and compensation based on the performance of that product against the plan. If the buyer brings in more product, and it sells through and exceeds the plan, then he or she receives a bigger bonus and is considered a huge success. However, here's where the risk comes in: If the buyer brings in product that doesn't sell, even by a comparatively small amount, he is penalized for over-ordering. Although this is frustrating to the toy company in question, you can't blame the buyer. Buying toys has a much greater risk than buying other products because you're actually putting your business in the hands of the whims of an 8-year-old, which are, as you might imagine, notoriously hard to predict.

The cost to the toy company and retailer in lost sales is potentially significant, though it's impossible to calculate the cost of inaction, other than to compare incremental sales in other channels and try to calculate what percentage it would be. You could do it, but it probably wouldn't change anything. In this case, the buyer's understandable and fully defensible self-interest is where the opportunity is lost. When the risk is too great, action stops, but in this case the action stops because the metrics of success don't support risk-taking, and in the case of the toy industry, buyers have been burned by irrational exuberance, as it were, because at the end of the day retail buying is far more an art than a science. A buyer who has been burned once, or who has made a bad decision, is going to be more careful.

And lest you think that this is limited to the toy industry, it's endemic to the entire retail industry in the current market. Why else do we see deep discounts in the last weeks before the Christmas holiday or post-holiday sales—or sales year-round, for that matter? In fact, we have an entire retail structure today that is designed to minimize risk. Sales executives consistently refer to buyers today as "risk managers," noting that at many retailers the buyer they are dealing with this year was buying in a totally different category six months ago. We hear all the time that buyers today are not merchants, which simply means that they don't have the in-depth experience of a category over time to know whether something has a good chance of working or not. In other words, they have no intuition and instead are forced to rely on spreadsheets and data that may or may not apply to a given product or product category.

I don't mean to jump all over retail buyers here. Those I've met are great people who earnestly want to succeed and do the best possible job, and quite frankly, more than a few seem to be at sea. If you're buying a commodity product one day that has a fairly predictable year-over-year performance and are thrown into a fashion business the next that is dependent on completely different consumer purchasing experience, what will you fall back on? You'll fall back on what you know and what has served you in the past, and in most cases that can be a data set or measurements that may not be appropriate for the challenges at hand.

Though I've used retailing as an example, you'll see this type of disconnect throughout businesses. What I'm talking about are the problems created by institutionalized systems that don't take into account the variations in different parts of a business.

The net result is that risk aversion kills innovation, certainly among some large companies because they are often so intent on hitting short-term goals in sales or revenue, often to please Wall Street and shareholders. Of course, there are many companies that invest in research and development (pharmaceuticals and chemicals spring to mind), but whether to invest or not in extensive R&D is a tough call for many companies. In the toy industry, though there have been changes in recent years, most companies are looking for others to do the research and development and even the initial sales prior to picking something up and taking it to the next level in terms of production and distribution.

There is still plenty of innovation happening at smaller companies, and it happens because people are passionate about an idea that they are putting into action, and their benchmarks are different. Most importantly, though, their approach to risk is different. The ability to play and see where the ideas take you—to take action within the parameters of a vision or a concept and the market, and without a benchmark that must be hit at all costs—is what can inspire truly play-full innovation.

Picking Your Playmates: Job-Hunting and Hiring

Answer this question as truthfully as you can: When you were in kindergarten, how long did it take you to figure out who you wanted to play with? Ten minutes? A couple of days? Maybe, if you were pushing it, a week?

When you started dating, how long did it take you to figure out if you wanted to go out with someone? Did you ever, as the song from *South Pacific* goes, "see a stranger across a crowded room" and know you wanted to know them better?

Humans are just naturally attracted to certain other humans for a lot of reasons we don't understand. Sure, you can sign on to a dating site and fill out a questionnaire, and let an algorithm pick a date for you. You can read about pheromones or the "art of attraction." There's even speed dating, which lets you meet a lot of people in a short time to see if something clicks. Or you can just meet people and get a sense that you like them and perhaps you want to see them again. What all of these have in common is that they reinforce that attraction is somewhat subconscious and a decision relatively quickly made.

One of my closest friends and I became friends, at least as I recall, in a very short time. At church school. In first grade. We grew up together and have stayed close our entire lives, all brought about by a few moments of play. Decades later we still enjoy each other's company and have a lifetime of memories and connection.

I bring this up because as I interview executives about work, I hear more stories about the difficulties and frustrations in identifying good candidates and hiring than any other single topic. Although this is only one part of running a business, it is also probably the best and most visceral indication of why and how the principles of play need to be applied in business today. The freedom to be oneself and draw on all of one's talents and experience in creating things, whether imaginary or tangible, is the essence of play. In the hiring process, we see what is perhaps the most human element of business—deciding who you want to play with—is being limited to data sets and risk aversion. The problem is, of course, that believing there is an absolutely perfect solution that is empirically demonstrable in such a sloppy and unpredictable area as human behavior is not merely the illusion that you can create a data set to know and predict something with as many unknowable variables as a human being; but that one also shortchanges and short-circuits one's own confidence and trust. This can start a cycle of doubt and distrust that feeds on itself and is the antithesis of play, which draws on all of what makes us human, both conscious and unconscious. I am in no way suggesting that you throw out data and information because, as discussed earlier, this is part of what feeds our choices—but only partially, because to be most effective, it has to be used in the context of a more comprehensive, creative, and yes, imaginative experience.

Because hiring is such a hot-button issue, it's a great example of what happens when the play, or human, elements are discarded. I hear tales of woe from both sides of the hiring desk. Applicants are baffled why it takes 13 interviews or more to be considered for a job, only to be turned down. Executives looking to hire say that they need to be sure they're making the right choice. Nobody wants to make a bad decision because it's expensive and can reflect poorly on the person making the decision, so the process becomes drawn out and great mountains of paper or megabytes of data are brought in to defend a choice. This is especially true at the higher levels where there are employment contracts, relocation, and other factors coloring the decision. But should it take 10 to 13 months to fill a vice president position? And does anyone calculate the costs related to that? We're not talking merely about the costs related to lost opportunity in the company of having a major gap in its management team. We're also talking about the cost to the applicants to take time off and pay for flights for initial interviews if they're not local, and the stress of waiting to hear, pass up other potential opportunities, and so forth.

Executive recruiter Amber Shockey, who specializes in the legal field, told me in an interview that she believes that the process really should be more like "looking for a friend on the playground." She says, though, that today the process can become complicated by the availability of too much information. When your pool of potential friends was limited to the other kids in your class, you had to make your choices based on what was available to you. This has been less true since the 1960s, when moving to take a job began to become more commonplace, through today, where the prevailing attitude is "I'll go where the job is," which is both the reality and the expectation today.

Shockey says that online services like LinkedIn can complicate the process, certainly for a recruiter, because the client will already have been through 100 profiles by the time she's called in. Additionally, she says that there is a prevailing belief that the perfect applicant can be identified statistically—that through the sheer force of data, it's possible to find the exact right person who fits the role. Shockey is not alone in this belief, but when did you ever create a spreadsheet to decide if you wanted to have coffee with someone? And don't tell me it's not the same thing; it is. We're talking about human connection here. Shockey adds that the belief that data can solve the problem can lead to information overload and the loss of the human element that's essential to any good hiring decision: "Clients want to see that I've called 100 people, and how those people replied. If I send them 25 prospective clients, they also want to know how another 25 responded." Shockey says that level of data is ultimately counter-productive and that the availability of raw information allows people to depend on data to give them the right answer. "It also means that companies believe that due to the plethora of information that's a few clicks away that they can see every possible candidate out there, so we have to find the best candidate out there," she says.

Of course, this is impossible in such a human business as hiring, and the volume of data provides a false sense of security that making a hiring decision can be quantified when it cannot. However, "all the left brain stuff has squashed the right brain," Shockey adds. What this also largely prohibits is a fluid hiring process or an ability to rethink what you want for a position based on applicants who may show up.

When I was involved in an interview process when I was still fairly young, I was interviewed by a marketing agency, and it was going pretty well, though I had the undefined feeling that there wasn't a great fit for me there, though I couldn't say why. At one point in my third interview, the person who would be my boss asked, "How hard do you work?"

"I don't understand the question," I replied.

"Well, we get here at 7 in the morning and we work till 7 at night" was the response. "Can you do that?"

"So, you're asking for a quantitative answer to a qualitative question," I asked. The interview ended pretty quickly thereafter, most likely to the satisfaction of both of us, and I wasn't offered the job. What I learned in that moment was nothing that can be quantified in data: that there probably wasn't a good fit between that company's culture and me. Several years later I had to interact with the company on another project, and my feeling was confirmed. The people I worked with were competent, personable, and good at their jobs, but they were very much convergent thinkers, whereas I tend to be more divergent in my approach. The company and I both dodged a bullet. To put this in terms of play as we've been discussing, after a few moments on the playground, we realized that we weren't going to become best friends and went our separate ways.

This was many years ago, and I was probably more arrogant than was appropriate, but in talking to executives who are searching for vice president positions and above, the desire to quantify a qualitative process is stronger than ever.

Shockey and others say that very often when companies are hiring, they want to find someone who has already done the job they're looking for—who hits "every bullet on the job description." The flaws in this should be obvious. You can't be playful or entertain other possibilities that might be beneficial if you're tied to a rigid job description. I have a close friend who has been single for several years, and is really eager to get into another relationship. However, she has a list of criteria that the prospective boyfriend has to fill, and if he doesn't, he's off the list. Some of these are practical and would be deal-breakers for anyone, such as no felony convictions or drug problems. Others, not so much—such as a sense of style and acceptable models of cars that he drives. I try to point out that she leaves very little room to be surprised by something unexpected this putative mate might bring to the table, or perhaps he drives an inexpensive car out of an approach to life and material possessions that she might find appealing or complementary, but she'll have none of it. And so, she keeps looking.

A senior executive we interviewed was in the running for the presidency of a privately held company in an industry that had, at most, four or five major players. After going through the initial interviews, getting through the headhunters and the HR people at the company, he finally began meeting the people who could make the hiring decision. Ultimately, the executive was one of three people still in the running for the job. He had been asked to create a strategic plan and a vision for the company for the next five years, which he did—without compensation, by the way. His proposal was full of charts and graphs, category analyses, and projections. It had taken a huge amount of time, and it's something that a company would have most likely paid a consultant tens of thousands of dollars to do. At the end of this process, the executive was told that he was the best candidate they had seen, but they weren't making an offer because he hadn't done this job before and didn't have direct industry experience. He had worked in related categories and had demonstrated an ability to expand lines and increase revenues, but he didn't have the one thing that would have made the CEO feel comfortable about hiring him. More than a year later, the job still isn't filled. Out of all the potential candidates out there, there may be only three or four who have that exact qualification, and they weren't looking to move.

This is the reality of the job-hunting market today, and it's not going to change overnight. In addition to scenarios like the previous one, we hear about having to get through a machine before even talking to a person. Optical scanning of resumes is a reality, but it's not necessarily a detriment. You can learn to create a more scanner-friendly resume (more active words, more words that indicate results, and so forth). You also have to deal with the reality of potentially making lateral moves and/or trying to move up in your company where you already have the relationships and the trust. It is a strategic game, and you owe it to yourself and your career to play it well. (See Chapter 9 for more on this.)

What you can't replace is the imaginative process. No machine can do that yet, just as no person is going to be everything you want. That's why you have a team of people to leverage the best of each one. Do you expect your spouse or partner to be *everything* to you? If you do, then you're bound to be disappointed because, quite frankly, no one can do that. In a relationship you say, "I love how he treats me, even if he does drop toothpaste in the sink." There always needs to be a version of that in business as well.

The two best hires I ever made didn't look right on paper. One, however, was one of the best marketing writers I had ever met, and I realized that she could learn our business easily, but what we needed most of all was a good writer. The other at age 30 was embarking on her third career. She had the basic skills we were looking for, but what she had that was most impressive was that she had demonstrably succeeded spectacularly in every job she'd had. The kind of person who is going to throw themselves passionately into the project was exactly what we needed; the rest could be learned. I'm happy to say that the first is extremely successful and still in the field. The second, after expanding the company in New York and opening an office in LA, because she rightly predicted growing opportunities there, decided she wanted to make documentary films, yet another new career. She's won several significant awards for her work. Neither of these people might look right on paper, and indeed, I had to fight my bosses to hire both, but I never regretted it, and we were successful and had a lot of fun along the way, even when things were difficult.

As Shockey says, if you're going to be effective in either hiring or looking for jobs, you can't allow information to suppress your gut feeling. If one is going to be completely honest, for all the data you collect, the final hiring decision is based on your imagination. You may be more informed about the person, you may be able to have information that allows you to make predictions in which you feel fairly confident, but can you really know? Of course not.

Your final decision is going to be based on how you imagine the person doing in the job. Just as when you accept a job, you imagine how you'll be in it. But as we continue to say, all reality—like all play—begins in the imagination. It may make you feel better to be able to say you "know," but really you're just imagining.

We don't have a solution, and we know that we're not going to be able to change entrenched policies and practices, but we do have a question. If you accept that your decision is significantly based on imagination, why not go for it, and imagine something bigger than you would have? At least experiment with taking your fear out of the mix and think of the possibilities. That's how play works.

Balancing Risk and Action

American naturalist John Burroughs said, "Leap and the net will appear." This has been appropriated by all kinds of people who use it in different styles of management training to encourage risk-taking. It's nice if you're trying to turn your office into a Zen sacred space or something along those lines. The saying also makes a very nice refrigerator magnet or a poster with a kitten or rainbow on it. But any child engaged in active play knows that if you leap without a plan, or a sense of what you're doing, you may splatter on the sidewalk—and that's true whether we're talking literally or metaphorically.

I know that what this saying is really trying to do is encourage people to trust their vision and belief in what they're doing. I'm definitely all for that. However, there is, or should be, a lot of looking before the leaping. Leaping too soon can undermine a workable idea. Leaping too late can mean a missed opportunity. And there are times when leaping is the only choice, and you have to hope for the best.

A few years ago, I was asked to consult for a woman who had established a company to sell the extract of a rare Andean cactus in Los Angeles. This extract was purported to have miraculous healing powers, which she had plenty of documentation to support. Red flag number one: None of the testimonials were medical, but because the supplement business is largely unregulated, and there were no plans to make medical claims, it could work. She had formed a company, and planned to position the extract as having shamanic powers that would cure the body and the spirit. It was actually a pretty cool story, if you buy that kind of thing, and there is a niche market that does. I have rarely encountered anyone so passionate about a business, but here's where she leapt too early: The cacti were extremely expensive, and she had driven nearly 300 of them back from Mexico, where she had bought them from a dealer, and had them on the patio of the house she was renting in West Los Angeles. The cacti were small and had to grow, which was the first part of her plan. (I didn't ask what they cost or how she got them through customs.) Passion, however, collided with practicality. With a large part of her capital tied up in the cacti, which she then had to keep alive, and no plan to be implemented, she was stuck. Meanwhile, the cacti died, as did the business. Clearly, this was someone who was willing to take a risk, but the risk was calculated incorrectly. Knowing when to take a major step back before you leap is an essential tool, and as passionate as you may be, you need to surround yourself with skeptics who will challenge you and keep you focused. Mine was actually the first questioning voice this woman had heard as we tried to structure a business from the various pieces she had. Ultimately, it didn't work.

In the mid-1980s, game designer Frank Coker created a game called The Next Empire. It was before the Internet, obviously, and, as Frank describes it, there were only two ways for people to play games together. One was the traditional way, which was to get a group of people together in a room to play. The other was a then-popular format, long forgotten now, called Play by Mail (PBM), games that ultimately evolved into Massive Multi-Player Online Games (MMOGs). Coker and his co-developers had invested huge amounts of time in developing the game, the mechanics, how to play, and the computer program that would calculate how players were doing. Each player would get a turn in the mail, which would take about three hours to complete. They would send it in, and the people running the game would put all the turns into the computer, and send back the results and what you needed for the next turn. The object of the game, as with most games of this nature, was to be the last ship left alive.

After nearly a year of development and extensive play testing, the game was two weeks away from production. Manuals (remember, this was the age of paper) were at the printers—and there was a glitch.

"We went through the last play test—a 'round-the-clock session from Friday to Sunday in a hotel suite—and a point came up that was fundamental to the game play. Almost unbelievably, it was one that hadn't come up in all the previous development and testing of the game," Coker told me when I interviewed him. "I was with all the other play testers, and we realized that if we changed this one point, it would be a better game. Changing it at the last minute, though, would be expensive, and there wasn't time to test this new variation. This is when your instincts and listening to people come into play because given the consensus that we would improve the game if we changed it, we went ahead."

Coker got the game to the trade show, and out into the market. And, as he says, against all odds and logic, it was named game of the year by one of the leading magazines covering Play by Mail games.

In taking this risk, Coker stresses that he was able to because of everything that had gone before in the development process. It was a crisis point in the project, and he says, "This is when both trusting your own instincts and listening to other people comes into play."

Creating a climate of intelligent risk is absolutely critical to move business ahead, particularly in the contemporary market. As times to market get shorter and competition gets stiffer and more cutthroat, markets become more narrowly defined and opportunities shorter; an ability to respond to changing dynamics becomes more critical than ever.

One of the most effective ways to do that is to surround yourself with people who will question everything—who will help you play out the story and consider various outcomes. This can be difficult in some work environments (as we'll discuss when we talk about business cultures), but it's critical. Coker and others stress the need to surround yourself with people who will challenge you. "I think it's more valuable for people to tell you what's wrong with your product than what's right," Coker says. "It's great to get the strokes and feel good about something you've done, but it's more necessary to hear what's wrong.

"And you can't argue. You need to take in the criticism and not argue. If people have problem with something, you had better listen. I go around continually during the design and development process and ask people to tell me what doesn't work, and then we constantly make adjustments. Many times I'm not happy with what doesn't work, but too bad."

In his situation, Coker had to take the action even in the face of significant risk. Not to make the change would have made the game less successful, and to wait until he had had the time to test the change would have missed the window. This is a situation where he leapt at the right time. If the net appeared when he leapt, it wasn't by magic; it was by drawing on the accumulated knowledge of the process and experience. That may be a little less romantic than magic, but it gives better odds of success.

Rethinking Failure

As I hope has become abundantly clear at this point, if we're going to successfully integrate the principles of play into more effective and innovative business, we have to rethink the concept of failure on a cultural basis. Yes, there are times when failure is bad—a Broadway show loses all its investment, a business crashes and burns, and so forth—but we're talking about financial failure in that context.

Active failure as a part of developing experience, as Coker describes, however, is a critical part of play. Failure is an inevitable part of the process, and as a culture, we need to understand the role of productive failure in the development process of anything we undertake. We need to reshape the conversation, to focus on what's learned in the process as a way to get to a result rather than each failure being interpreted as bad because it didn't get the result on the first try. As noted, what kid really expects that?

However, we live in a culture that permeates business as well, where the emphasis is on the result rather than the process. Too often we teach children that failure is somehow a defect not of action but of character, and this instills risk aversion almost from the cradle.

But if you think about it, more things fail than succeed, as we've described. If you're willing to ask "What if?" you have to be open to the possibility that the answer isn't what you're hoping.

Just as we've defined what winning is so we know if we've done it, we also need to define failing in the same way. Like the kid working on perfecting that skateboard jump, we have to see failure as exciting, informative, and inspiring.

What You Can Do

1.	Give your gut a little more credence. We're not saying bet the farm based on a hunch, but we are saying trust the wealth of knowledge you've developed over time and that your amazing brain can access.
2.	Don't hide behind data to justify doing what you want to do anyway. It's definitely part of the equation, but human decisions are made by humans, not by algorithms. There is no algorithm in the world that is as powerful as your experience.
3.	Put the emphasis on process. Build time to fully develop concepts and test them so they work.
4.	Ask what's wrong more than you ask what's right, and listen.
5.	Acknowledge that failure is more common than success in human endeavors and embrace it as a valuable part of the process.

Drop It if It Doesn't Work

Have you ever seen a kid spend hours or days trying to make a toy, scenario, or activity that is clearly unprofitable and not fun, work? I didn't think so.

Kids simply don't spend time with things that they don't enjoy and that aren't workable. (We're going to make a natural exception for anything that takes time to master like a musical instrument or a sport, but that practice is built in to the activity from the outset.) There are many reasons why a toy doesn't work for a kid: lack of interest, too complicated, not a good fit with their play style, not as fun as they anticipated. When there isn't a compelling reason or tangible incentive to stick with something, kids drop it and move on to the next thing. Moreover, they spend very little time analyzing why something isn't working. They move on to the next thing. There is no ego involved. No recrimination. Nothing. It's done.

So, why do adults do it? There are a bunch of reasons, but before we get into those, ask yourself how often you've considered something a "fool's errand." "Beating a dead horse"? Or, in Hamlet's somewhat more poetic phrasing, "weary, stale, flat and unprofitable"?

The amount of time and money lost from forcing products into the market, investing in projects long past their viability, or engaging in activities that won't fulfill objectives has never been measured. It's doubtful whether or not it can be, but we certainly know anecdotally from interviews with executives at a variety of companies that waste and investment long after a project should be dropped are common occurrences. Nor is this phenomenon limited to private companies, driven by perhaps an idiosyncratic owner with a vision.

As a start, consider these three scenarios:

- An outdoor products company decides that it wants to expand into lifestyle products. They hire staff, design products, produce prototypes, and even when they get a lackluster response go into production. A year later, the new division is shuttered, the investment is lost, and all the new hires are back on the street.

- The owner of a mid-sized children's products company has a dream in which he sees a fashion doll line with a story about girls that transform into cats. Though the company has never made dolls before, they push them into production. At the same time, they introduce a technology that allows the dolls to interact with on-screen games. They get initial placement at toy retailers, but in the highly competitive fashion doll market, they are quickly overwhelmed and don't even last one season.

- A publicly traded company spends more than $7 million on a one-time, one-day promotion for a successful product that has a 79-cent-per-unit wholesale cost for the major products in its line. The promotion is, as you might expect, very dramatic and even gets some national TV coverage. Apparently, though, no one points out that the company would have to sell an incremental 9.1 million units in order to make the promotion pay for itself.

In each of these scenarios, there were surely moments at which red flags should have been waving wildly where someone should have put on the brakes. But they did not. As my father used to say of our rector's sermons, "He reached three perfectly good stopping points, and went right on through them."

Of course, hindsight may be clear, but it's not particularly useful unless it can inform other efforts moving forward. What is it that kids know that adults have forgotten—or choose to ignore—that might help make better choices?

For one, when something isn't working for a kid, as noted at the beginning of the chapter, they have no ego engaged in dropping it. Certainly that's not true in many business situations. We hear time and time again from frustrated executives about pet projects that come around not through analysis but because the "big boss" wants to do it. They're afraid to challenge something, even when their promotions or bonuses may depend on the success or failure of a project.

The problem is that no one wants to call an ego-driven project what it is. No one wants to tell the emperor that he's naked. Instead, people jump through hoops to try to rationalize something, call in research, and generate mounds of data that support the project. At a certain point, since it appears something is going to be done anyway, people throw in the towel and try to make the best of it. In such situations, the goal often becomes to mitigate damage, spin the results, and try not to be blamed for any disaster. This creates a fear-driven and defensive environment where the objective becomes to save one's skin rather than move it forward.

Just before the Internet crash in 2000, we were consulting to a company that had raised a boatload of money on the speculation that their business proposition would revolutionize online job-hunting. Our research pointed out the flaws in the process from a human stand-point, but the CEO, who was besotted with technology, asserted that it would be so exciting that people would adapt to using the technology. He rejected the research, referred to our team as "analog," a seemingly scathing criticism at the time, and pushed ahead with the project. Further testing of the system validated our questions, and the whole project crashed and burned spectacularly, one of the casualties of that particular time. The cost of the loss was far greater than the cost of pulling back and retooling based on the information we had about how people wanted to do research on jobs and job functions.

(People will adapt to new ways of doing things. Just look at the rise of online shopping, but that happened over time. It is very rare that one product will change consumer behavior, the obvious exceptions being the iPod, iPhone, and iPad. But the rarity of their success and the industries they spawned prove the point that the truly revolutionary is not an everyday experience.)

Several years later, we tested a product concept for a major luxury goods company wanting to get into the broader collectibles market with a comparatively low-end offering at about $50. Though the concept tested well with many populations and in different regions where the parent company was established, it quickly became clear that it could not be produced at a cost that would work within its target market segment, and that the overall market based on the price was substantially smaller than projections and what was needed to make a viable product. There were many other reasons to suggest going back to the drawing board or even tabling the project, but that was at odds with what the people driving the product within the company wanted. A crisis of sorts occurred, but if you've been following along so far, you can probably guess that, against all the information and against the odds, they pushed ahead with the product. Once produced, it got some placement and actually sold a few pieces. On the whole, though, the product was a failure, and it was only the size of the parent company that allowed it to absorb the loss relatively easily. (Being a private company doesn't hurt, either.)

This is where ego comes into play: More is at stake than whether something works or doesn't work, and that's the problem. The person who is supposed to be a visionary has an investment in making something work against all odds, and that opens the door to bad decision-making. The volatile, inter-personal dynamics at the luxury goods company created a political situation that ultimately wasn't about making or not making a product. It was about proving a point. This type of political situation can be all too common, and what should be rational, dispassionate decisions about the viability of an initiative become clouded by personal investment. We're all people, and on some level we're all passionate about certain things, but keeping an eye on the larger objectives, or having someone who can rein in the egos, is essential to creating a success. This type of behavior is more pronounced in private and very often family-run businesses, although it still happens in large companies as well.

Companies are often also hesitant to drop something that isn't working because the project has passed a supposed "point of no return." This is the point at which so much has been invested in time, money, materials, and so forth, that it's impossible to pull the plug.

The argument we hear about this point is that, sure, kids can drop something if it doesn't work because they have no investment in it. Mom or Dad, or someone, bought the toy, so there's no financial risk, and it's easy to find something else. That's not exactly true, and once again it's the application of an adult's understanding and interpretation of experience to a child's reality. All you have to do is talk to a kid who has been disappointed by something he or she hoped to get for a birthday or holiday and you'll see this is, from a child's perspective, quite serious. They might wish they had asked for something quite different.

The real issue for adults is that the prevailing belief that dropping something is failure. Discovering something you believed in doesn't work the way you hoped is failure. The situations in which a company has held back something or delayed a launch are often considered failures. And failure is to be avoided at all costs because it reflects negatively on the individual or the company and invalidates them on a very elemental level. So we hear the argument "Well, we've invested X dollars in it, so we need to see it through."

"They'll think there's something wrong with the product" is something we also hear a lot when there are indications that a launch should be delayed. Well, of course there's something wrong with the product. If there weren't, why on earth would you hold it back? Even a publicly held company might do better taking a hit on its stock for delaying a product than on lost revenue from rushing something into the market. (And they might not even suffer that, if they frame the story correctly.)

But how do you *know* if something isn't going to work? Or isn't working? That's really one of the questions. Sure, you say, a kid knows because all he or she has to deal with is his or her feeling at the moment. Well, sure, we're taking a little poetic license, but there are ways to know—and indications along the way.

Recently, a small, privately held toy company held back a major new launch for a full year because they thought the product needed more development. It's not that there weren't orders or interest from retailers, but the product wasn't working the way they wanted it to, and they knew a little more time in development could solve that problem. They were willing to take the short-term financial hit in order to take the chance on being more successful and profitable when the product finally came out. The product actually did very well when it was introduced and exceeded projections. Would it have been as profitable if it had been introduced on its original timetable? Impossible to tell. Nonetheless, the product's ultimate success was what mattered, and the risk paid off.

What these situations really require are structures that allow for fluidity and response to new information and changing conditions. As we've said—but it bears repeating here—kids trying to master a skateboard trick fail much more than they succeed. The same is true in business. For every hit product or every successful initiative, there are many that don't make it. Like the kid on a skateboard, you have to be comfortable with risk and think of the process as one that's going to have bumps and setbacks. As the oft-quoted, and perhaps apocryphal, saying from Thomas Edison goes, "I haven't failed to make a light bulb. I've successfully found 1,000 ways that didn't work."

Kids can also drop something if it doesn't work for them because they have all the information they need based on their personal tastes, play styles, and experience to determine if they want to continue with something or not.

Obviously, this is not as simple with business ventures or adults, but the principle still merits consideration. Whereas kids have merely their own pleasure to consider, businesses must consider the market, investment to date, projected return, their audience, competition, and so forth.

So, we have market research. This is, for the most part, how you're going to "know" whether or not something is working. In an ideal world, research helps you determine if something is working, or what it needs to work, or whether, in fact, you should drop it. It can be invaluable—if it's used correctly.

The problem that we see with research, however, is that too often it's not well structured or designed to achieve a specific outcome, or the data is misinterpreted.

Too often we see research used as cover for when things don't work. "Our research said 'X,' so we were surprised when the product failed" is something we often hear in post-mortem sessions. This is like a kid trying to deflect blame by saying another kid told him to do something.

"What went wrong with the research?" is a question that's seldom asked. Well, generally what went wrong is the research was manipulated to give a desired result. This is called bias confirmation. Or the research wasn't structured to give a clear answer. The sample might not have been large enough or diverse enough. Or, more often than not, it hasn't been considered in a broad enough context, so what appears to be definitive information isn't an accurate picture.

A major bank was trying to figure out how to refine its credit card marketing targeting college students—already a complicated and somewhat controversial issue. Four focus groups in four cities indicated that college freshman really didn't understand how credit cards worked. The creative team came back with three treatments, and the one that emerged from qualitative testing as being most appealing to students was produced. The campaign featured a puzzle and included copy about finding your way through the confusing world of credit cards.

The campaign failed. Big time. In fact, it was such a disaster, compared to their previous campaigns, that the managers had to put the failed creative back into focus group testing to find out why, especially when compared to campaigns that had worked. The results revealed that students still thought credit was confusing, but they didn't need to be told that. They needed to be given a simple solution, which, by the way, is what the successful campaign continued to do.

The point of this story is that in trying to save money, the bank missed an opportunity to find out if something was or wasn't going to work—while there was still time to drop or fix it.

What this points to is that focus groups can be effective, but they are also misleading. Show consumers a new product, and they'll likely be interested. Adult focus group participants love the attention and generally try to be helpful. Kid focus groups in the toy industry are notoriously inconclusive, because if you put a child in the room with a new toy he or she hasn't seen, engagement is a given.

There's also another problem with a lot of research: By the time a company engages in it, development is so far along that it seems impossible to turn back, and whether consciously or unconsciously, the research is structured to provide a predetermined response, so despite the investment of time and expense, no one really wants an answer that's going to challenge what was going to happen anyway. In the case of the campaign mentioned previously, which was to be delivered via direct mail, of the three treatments tested it emerged as the best, but by that time the bank was committed to doing one of them. What they were testing was the execution of an idea rather than the communication overall. The research was flawed because the outcome—producing one of the three treatments—was a foregone conclusion.

Companies invest a lot in research. Good research is hugely expensive, is time-consuming, and has precise rules for methodology if you want real insights, rather than validation. Moreover, even statistically defensible research can never tell you definitively if something will work. There are way too many variables to ever test all of them reliably, and in a dynamic marketplace, research is a snapshot of one point in time. However, even less than perfectly structured research *can* tell you that something will not work. And it's probably good to pay attention when that happens.

Even with the best research, there are no guarantees, and there are going to be times when things don't work for reasons that are difficult if not impossible to determine. Unlike the child who can simply drop something and move on, most business situations required an exit strategy.

This is something that we're seeing more and more as a result of a fragmented economy and consumer behavior that is increasingly difficult to predict and/or quantify.

If you're completely gung-ho about a new product, it can seem like a buzzkill to have to go in with a strategy for what you'll do if your product doesn't work, but more and more retailers are making it an essential element of any sale. They want to know what you plan to do if something fails to perform and how to mitigate potential damages to all concerned. And exit strategies force you to ask tough questions, which, when done well, can only help you gather more information.

A good exit strategy considers all the variables and projects actions you can take. Nobody wants to assume something is going to fail, but if you're considering the exit at the outset, it can help you temper your plans and be able to scale down—or if all goes well, scale up—your plans as you go along. Moreover, it's not just the final exit strategy that you should be concerned about. As you develop plans, think of your project as a turnpike with exit points along the way. Each of these presents an opportunity to make choices and, most importantly, keep an objective eye on whether or not something is working. You don't have to take the exit, but you should be cognizant of having a choice, to hyperextend the metaphor.

This, ultimately, is what happens when individuals or companies push forward with things long after a point of viability. They've come to believe that they have no choice in the matter, and they're stuck with what they've got. That's almost never true, and it's often beneficial to consider an exit strategy, and when to implement that exit strategy when it's clear something isn't working. This can often be challenging and politically difficult, particularly when people have egos invested in a project, but it's also responsible to admit the possibility that something might not work and create a contingency plan. This is going to be more and more prevalent a practice, as marketing becomes more data-driven and that data is almost instantaneously available. In other words, you'll know pretty soon if something isn't working.

What You Can Do

1.	Don't shortchange the time in the information-gathering stage.
2.	Do test early and test often to the extent that you can. An investment in research can save time and money.
3.	Don't discard well-structured research if it doesn't give you the answer you want. That's an opportunity you shouldn't ignore.
4.	Do consider cost/benefit analysis for everything you undertake. This is not always a financial analysis, but do create measurement criteria. (Don't trap yourself in a situation where you have to sell more than a year's worth of incremental merchandise to pay for a one-day promotion—that is, unless you can quantify it another defensible way.)
5.	Don't let your ego get the best of you. We all hate to see things we love fall by the wayside, but if it's evident that something isn't going to work, short-term disappointment is better than a long-term mess.

Playing the Game

When you come right down to it, Mary Poppins knew an awful lot about how to get things done. As she sang, "You find the fun, and snap! The job's a game." For children cleaning up their rooms, turning the chore into a game makes the work go faster. And that's a child's game. But, to continue the metaphor, children play Candyland, and adults play Risk. Where children are content with the luck of the dice—and an occasional dip in the chocolate swamp—adult games are infinitely more elaborate and strategic. For adults, the way the game is structured and played determines the outcome. A lucky roll of the dice can help, but it is not the sole determining factor of who wins and who loses.

The same elements that make a good game also provide the strategic framework for competing in today's marketplace. (This is especially true in a market and a marketing-driven culture that is as dynamic and mercurial as our own.) Games, like business, require a fundamental concept, clear objectives, and a set of rules. So far, that's pretty obvious.

Good games also have three other things in common that are essential to their success: They have clear objectives, are easy to learn, and are different depending on who is playing them. These are significant features. We've discussed the necessity of clear objectives earlier, but what bears repeating in the context of games is that if you have no idea what winning is, you're not going to be able to plan a way to achieve your objectives, or know when you have won.

When we're talking about "easy to learn" with respect to games, what we're really talking about is clarity. Someone can pick it up and know exactly what they need to do. It's not over-thought and it's not overly complex. When I worked on launching the game Pictionary, we had one line: "It's charades on paper." This really tells you all you need to know. There may be details that require clarification, but the overall concept is delivered in a simple, comprehensible way that's accessible to everyone.

Linda Pezzano, who was a marketing mastermind and with whom I worked at Pezzano and Company, launched Trivial Pursuit as well as Pictionary and, always believed in the power of simplicity in communication. Even in the mid-1980s, she saw how difficult it was to get the attention of people, a challenge that's only escalated in the ensuing years. She believed that effective communication boiled things down to their essence to get consumers intrigued. Once their interest had been piqued, you had to be ready to provide more information, but at that time, she believed, the balance of power in the interaction had changed. It shifted from you as the marketer trying to get attention to your prospect wanting to know more. Sometimes weeks were spent developing that simplicity for clients—such as those in wastewater management—or they came in a flash of inspiration, but Linda always boiled it down to a game and to finding that thing that would make someone want to play with you. She was equally adamant that the role of the marketer was to be the catalyst for someone's experience and that it couldn't be forced on people, particularly when, as with a game, what you're selling is not essential to survival and is in a competitive market.

In the final analysis, what this means is that you have to both simplify the message and give people what we call a "way in"—a way to project themselves into an experience that they want to have. In toys and play, this doesn't just apply to board games; it applies to all sorts of toys. If the toy or game is too complex, and if it doesn't engage the individual or the imagination, it's not going to work over the long term. We tend to call these "watch me" toys. These are toys that do what they do whether or not someone is playing with them. We always say, you can start it up, go have a sandwich, and the toy just keeps going. That's certainly one kind of toy, and the global success of Tickle Me Elmo would certainly attest to the fact that this can work, but it's not a long-term strategy because ultimately when you leave out the kid who's supposed to be playing with it, they'll get bored. Remember: Kids, like consumers, are nothing if not completely self-involved. Your job, really in almost any function, is to get people to want to play with you, and that has as much to do with them and their perceptions as it does with what you do or say.

So, once you've got them hooked, your next task is to overcome the inevitable resistance that will come up. Let's look at Pictionary again for how this can work. It's all very well and good to get people intrigued by the idea of "charades on paper," but almost as quickly as people got the concept, they think, "But I can't draw." The fun of the game is that it doesn't matter if you can draw or not, and someone who takes a long time to draw well might be at a disadvantage. The fun of the game is really about how well people communicate.

This brings me to the most important element of the three features mentioned: The game is different depending on who is playing. This is critical at all levels of business, but it really comes down to the very simple concept of knowing your audience. Whether you're communicating internally or marketing, it's important to know who you're talking to as well as you can. We often call this "speaking into their hearing." The essential element of this is that people will always hear you through their filters, so analyzing those is important to your ultimate success. It's important that you not end up talking to yourself.

If you're making up the game, which is what you do as a business-person, the focus needs to be on the players. Lose that focus or misread the players, and your brand is likely to get stale and lose share.

This is exactly what happened with Mattel's Barbie and MGA's Bratz. Bratz were launched in 2001 with a dramatically different look than any previous fashion doll, and a marketing platform that was aggressive and reflected the kind of edgy fashions that were very much of the moment. It was the antithesis of Barbie. Novelty, however, was only part of what drove the doll's success. What really changed was how the game was played. Whereas Barbie's design and marketing always sought the implicit or even explicit support of parents, which it could do given its history, Bratz went directly to kids, knowing that what kids asked for, parents would buy. And it worked, for a time. The game had changed, and whatever one might think of it, marketing to kids worked, and it went beyond product and challenged the role of the parent in the purchase of fashion dolls for kids.

But that's not the end of the story. Bratz ultimately died down significantly, partially because the game changed again. Given that the toy market is always changing as new kids enter it—and the rate of change is much faster than other market sectors—a new group of parents looked at the Bratz and were upset at what they thought was the sexualized nature of the dolls. This issue, combined with the dolls not seeming novel to a new group of kids who wanted something new that was uniquely theirs, meant there was a different group playing the game, to continue our metaphor, and the company did not respond well. Barbie, after some defensive missteps such as launching a direct Bratz competitor called Flavas, focused on creative entertainment and other elements that were certainly within the context of the Barbie brand legacy but resonated with new groups of girls and moms, and regained market share.

The point of this is to illustrate how quickly the game can change in this market. As noted, it's probably faster in the toy industry than in some commodity businesses, but the principle is the same. Elsewhere we've discussed the importance of research and its effective uses, but research must always be analyzed and interpreted in the context of the larger culture. Too often we see companies that take qualitative research and look at it in isolation. The game is bigger than that, and you have to be thinking several moves ahead. As we always say, research is helpful, but it's only a snapshot of a moment in time. You have to consider all the pieces on the board or you're likely to be in trouble.

The Importance of Rules

Even if you're making up the game, there are rules you have to follow. You can't play Harry Potter or Batman or G.I. Joe or even Barbie without some parameters on the play. Monopoly isn't Monopoly unless it's played by the rules of the game.

We're not talking about rules in terms of laws or regulations. We're going to assume you—or someone you work with—have all of that under control. When we talk about rules in the perspective of play, we're talking about the boundaries and structures that define the game. In the culture, these are the forces that shape belief systems and perceptions.

These can be societal or religious or philosophical, and they can be quite confusing and at times conflicting. But they are an essential organizing principle for groups of people. What's particularly challenging to marketers and businesses right now is the fragmentation of the marketplace and the number of diverse rules one has to consider in talking to them. These rules become perpetuated by stories, and form the identity for a company or an individual or a group.

From a marketing or business perspective, rules also create an identity. Most companies have an identifiable culture, and the people who thrive there have internalized the rules of that culture or are likely to leave. Finding that match is critical in hiring because, though somebody may be perfectly competent and experience, if they don't fit into the culture of a company, they're not going to play well with others, and over the long term will likely be less effective.

Brands also function in the consumer's mind on a set of rules. As we discussed, a brand is a story that the consumer has come to believe in. Tide gets clothes cleaner, Crest gets teeth whiter, and so forth. To the consumer story is the fundamental truth of the brand, and the rules are what reinforce that truth over time because they are what give the brand its identity and dependable consistency.

Obviously, this might seem limiting on the surface. You can't really do much with Tide and Crest, other than update the formula. You can't make Fritos taste like something entirely different, because if you break the rules, you've broken the essential contract with the consumer, which is a dependable, predictable experience.

Except when you can.

In a competitive environment where retailers are risk-averse and competition is high, your rules can actually be a strategic jumping-off point, at least if your approach to your brand is outward-looking.

Consider the Jeep brand: How it went from the battlefield to the backyard is a great story for anyone looking to expand a brand. The vehicles were first created in World War II and, like many things developed for the war effort, found a place in civilian life back in the United States after the war. The brand's legendary toughness and performance under challenging conditions became the brand's identity. In the ensuing years, Jeep became a family car, but it always kept its identity as rugged and individual. The rule of the brand, if you will, was that it stood for anything rugged, outdoors, and adventurous. That eventually became a characteristic people wanted to associate themselves with, and so they began buying other products that were branded Jeep. And so, a Jeep stroller is assumed to be rugged, be dependable, and convey a sense of adventure. If you analyze it too closely, it doesn't make a whole lot of sense, and surely the soldiers who drove the first Jeeps around the battlefields of Europe would probably not have believed their "Blitz Buggies" would inspire a baby buggy, but in the world of strategic brand evolution overtime, it was inspired. If we define the game as interactions with the Jeep brand, over time the players changed from soldiers to civilians, but the civilians wanted to align their identities with the brand's story of ruggedness and individuality. This is fundamental to the adoption of any brand, naturally. There is very little objective relationship between a solider driving a Jeep in a war zone and a parent pushing a stroller in a shopping mall, but subjectively and perhaps even subconsciously the brand comes to complement part of the consumer's internalized identity. That is one of the most powerful elements a brand can have, and the expansion of the rules to include that modern mall denizen opens up new markets and opportunities without violating the brand's core rules, which are arguably its greatest asset, because the rules stimulate the story the consumer tells him- or herself. To get there, however, the brand managers had to be willing to play around with the brand, and to continually revise and update the story to reflect a changing consumer (and the realities they were creating). What once seemed illogical has made perfect sense (and significant profits) because, over time, play has allowed the rules to change.

When the Game Changes Radically

There are always game-changing events that you have to adapt to in an ongoing way. But sometimes there are events that create wholesale, seismic change that affects individuals and businesses by creating a radically altered game. Moveable type, radio, and TV spring to mind in the annals of communication. But no change has been as fast or as transformative as the rise of the Internet. With TV and radio, communication and advertising changed over time, but the basic premises of the business did not. Companies sold products. They told people about them in creative ways, and people either bought them or they didn't.

The online world, though, has changed the dynamics of business in a way that we haven't seen before. What used to be a one-way conversation between a company and a customer has become a dialogue—and not always a very nice one at that. Everyone with a keyboard and a connection is a critic and can potentially influence business. And everyone with a camera can become a star. Measurement metrics, writing to maximize search engine operations, the availability of information, and the speed of response and interaction are transforming everything from politics to pornography.

But even as dramatically as functions and communications have been transformed, not everything is changed. Marketing expert and agency owner Jennifer Deare noted to me in an interview:

There are basic human factors that drive business that really don't change over time. How those are experienced and expressed, however, is changing today at an ever-faster pace. The challenge facing every business right now in terms of leveraging the Internet, is to figure out how to understand the changing nature of communication, purchasing and consumption structures, but not leave behind the essential element of marketing and business which is the ability to make a connection between a person's identity and the expression of that identity through what they buy and the experiences they seek.

When a new game emerges—which is really what the online world is—this is when the principles of play matter the most. After all, a common element of all play with kids is knocking over the blocks and building again. You've been presented with some brand new pieces, and you need to put them together in a way that works in a different way.

The companies we work with that are using the Internet effectively are those that have been willing to re-examine their business in light of this new information. They are creating new models, for instance, for research and interpreting data. They are monitoring interactions with their consumers and responding to comments online, and they are engaged in a process of re-invention that is the essence of play. Moreover, they are embracing the fact of non-stop change and responding to it. They are looking for or, in some cases, creating the new rules to accommodate the new game, and at the same time leveraging and preserving that which has worked in the past.

This is where imagination and play count most; it's where you are free to create something new in response to a changing and developing world.

What You Can Do

1.	Turn the focus outward. If you are working in a consumer business, your consumer and his or her perceptions, reality, and concerns are paramount. Make sure you're not talking to yourself.
2.	Analyze your business in this light. Make sure that you know what all the explicit and implicit "rules" are about your company.
3.	Don't leave your customers' evolving interaction with your company or product or brand out of the strategy as you seek to expand.
4.	Realize in this market that the rules are changing faster than ever before. Make sure your company is structured to be responsive.
5.	Rethink failure. It's your best source of information. And while you're at it, agitate for this on a cultural basis.

Get Playing

What makes good, productive play? Well, that's going to be different for every person involved. Over the years, we've observed thousands of kids engaged in play, and although there are certainly many commonalities, and the developmental functions and benefits of play are clear, every play event is different because every child is different. There have been billions of Barbie dolls sold, but when you get past the reality of inert polyvinylchloride, which is what Barbie literally is, every Barbie doll is unique because it's brought to life in the imagination at a different time by a different person.

By definition because it is unstructured and not always clearly defined, some play is inherently chaotic and non-linear. In the imagination, it balances reality with flights of fancy to open up all kinds of possibilities. Seemingly contradicting that notion is that some play is focused and directed. Kids, as we've consistently observed over the years, naturally move between these two styles of play. When we ask kids about the toys they play with, there is generally a mix of types of toys. In fact, we often talk about "the balanced toy box," which posits that kids need and thrive on different types of play as they are developing at different times of life. This is especially true in the preschool and early grade-school years when parents and caregivers are more supportive of diverse, non-productive play experiences.

As kids become socialized outside the home, however, we also observe that they tend to group organically with kids who have similar play styles. This obviously makes sense because, as we discussed earlier, companionship is an integral part of play and part of developing an individual identity within the context of a group.

Naturally, though, what's possible in a self-selecting cohort on the playground is not possible in a business. Though you will develop friendly relationships at work—or at least I hope you do, because it's so much more fun to work with people you enjoy seeing—you may have very little voice in selecting your, pardon the expression, playmates. So if you're a manager and you sometimes feel like a kindergarten teacher, that's inevitable. If you're working and you sometimes feel like you're back in high school dealing with a clique, well, that's probably exactly right, too. That's human nature, and it doesn't change, so you might as well embrace it and have a good laugh at yourself on the way. The one advantage adults have over kids is perspective based on experience. And, as we discussed earlier, that's the value of play to help create experiences and imagine outcomes in a safe environment that you can try out later. One of the tactics we often find is very useful in trying to solve conflicts is listening to how the people describe the situation and then thinking of it in playground terms because what we find is that people's play styles don't change. I want to stress that we don't do this overtly, because people tend to get ticked off when you suggest they're behaving like a child on a playground. (Go figure!) But it can give you some insights into the way people act and are likely to interact.

5 Playground Types

If people get touchy when you tell them they're acting like children, they get downright cantankerous when you tell them they fit a specific type. So my strong suggestion when it comes to this type of stuff is that you do what any brilliant 1-year-old would do: Sit back and observe. There is a prevailing sensitivity in our culture at present to putting people into types because it is often perceived to invalidate them as individuals. People are complex and unique, but they do also fit into types. We're not going to delve into the psychological causes of these types; we'll leave that to the psychologists (and quite frankly, kids on a playground couldn't care less why a person is the way they are; they just have to deal with them—or not).

All sensitivities aside, types are a part of any society. Ask any casting director, and they will tell you that what they look for first are types. Indeed, the first part of any casting call is getting "typed out." It works like this: A group of people is lined up across the stage, and the casting people select the first ones that match the type they're looking for, and the rest get sent home without getting to speak Shakespeare or sing Sondheim. The ability to determine types based on experience is hard-wired into us, and we automatically look for visual cues about someone when we first encounter them. Those cues can be shaped by our experiences and, in some cases, neuroses, but they're still there. Pretending those cues either aren't there or not to pay attention to them as part of the information you're taking in, is to deny an important component of your personality.

That said, let's look at a handful of playground types and how you might play better with them. This list is neither comprehensive, nor does it explore all the different nuances of relationships with these types, but hopefully it will give you some ideas as either teacher or classmate (manager or co-worker) for making the most of those relationships. As with every system of classification, the vast majority of people will not fit neatly into one of these types, but they will most likely have dominant characteristics that are identifiable by the type.

It's also important to note before we jump into this that there can never be any defense for someone whose behavior or language is inappropriate or in violation of personnel policies, and those must be dealt with through established channels in your business. For all the romance of the TV show, this is not the *Mad Men* era, and there can be no tolerance at any level of an organization for abuse of any kind. What we're talking about here are the inherent traits of these types and how you might handle them.

The Bossy Kid

The Bossy Kid on the playground. We'll start here because a lot has been written about this lately, mostly in terms of gender. Men who are domineering, demanding, and directive are supposedly respected, whereas girls or women are told they're "bossy" as a criticism. That's a societal construct about how boys and girls "should" be. Being bossy isn't really gender-specific. We've seen bossy kids of both genders and their behaviors are consistent. On the playground, these are kids who tell others what to do, who are, in fact, demanding, and who like to run the show. They'll often get into conflict when challenged, and are more likely to quit an activity if they're not in control. These kids are primarily convergent thinkers who are probably not motivated by malice. Rather, they believe that they have the best way to play and that they're way is going to be the most fun for everyone. Their flaw is that they can't see how their behavior affects everyone else, and they are also more likely to take their ball and go home when things don't go their way.

The Bossy Kid at work. This is the person who is organizing everything from meetings to the football pool. The positive side is that the

Bossy Kid really helps get things done, and is the person you want managing a process because he or she is often very detail intensive, and things aren't going to slip. His or her identity is based on being in charge. The downside is that the Bossy Kid can tend to be a micromanager, and he or she can dominate meetings and be unreceptive to ideas that he or she hasn't come up with. The Bossy Kid is also less likely to take responsibility when things go wrong, which can be problematic.

If you work for a Bossy Kid. The good news is that you probably never have to worry about forgetting anything, because your Bossy Kid will be on top of you all the time. This can be good if you're not one yourself, but if you are, you may have conflict. The best advice we have is always to pick your battles and make sure that you're clear about the plan of action. Providing regular updates tends to mollify the Bossy Kid and let him or her know that things are progressing. When there are problems, the Bossy Kid will want to be actively involved in the solution. You won't have as much autonomy as working with another type, and clear communication is going to be essential, particularly if you need to track back to find the source of an error.

If you work with a Bossy Kid. This can be exasperating, as the Bossy Kid tends to dominate meetings, and is highly opinionated in brainstorming and other meetings. The Bossy Kid also tends to be problematic in a team setting and can often be resistant to new ideas. The Bossy Kid who doesn't get his or her way is the one sitting with arms crossed over his or her chest withdrawing from participating in a meeting. Fortunately, most managers with a lick of sense recognize this pattern, so you probably don't need or want to do anything about it. However, if you want to score points in that situation, toss an idea back to the Bossy Kid for his or her opinion. He or she will be happy to be heard, whether or not the resulting ideas are implemented. You're not going to change him or her, but there's no profit in creating or maintaining conflict tension. One of the things we always ask kids who are in conflict with Bossy Kids is whether they'd rather be right or get along and play? It probably costs you little or nothing to be nice, and conflict is always best avoided.

The Kinetic Kid

The Kinetic Kid on the playground. This is the kid who can't sit still—who is jumping on and off the swings, climbing the monkey bars, running around like a crazy person. This kid has a lot of energy that he or she needs to burn off, and that shows up in virtually non-stop action. The positive side is that this kid is a font of ideas. He or she is pretty much the definition of the divergent thinker who can jump from idea to idea with sometimes blinding speed. The positive part of this type is that he or she is almost always engaged and wants to engage others too. He or she is what my mother used to call a "perpetual motion machine."

The Kinetic Kid at work. This type is always coming up with new ideas and never stops, and very often the ideas can make the project better, even if they make the work more difficult or complex. That's also the downside of this type. You can feel whipsawed from idea to idea, and it can be hard to get things done. The Kinetic Kid is like a terrier that is adorable but needs attention all the time. He or she may also have few social filters, which can be endearing and amusing within reason, but also be problematic when it's not controlled. Like the terrier, however, the Kinetic Kid is always looking for attention and tends to be very responsive to feedback and correction, and rarely takes it personally.

If you work for a Kinetic Kid. Prepare to be interrupted; that's just the way it goes. This can be a very exciting person to work for. You'll never be at a loss for new thinking or new ideas, and this type can be very inspiring. Every day can feel like an ongoing brainstorming session, and this type tends to be extremely passionate about the job. The challenges come with the interruptions. It may be difficult to find time to focus or plan, and you may feel that projects veer off in different direction, because of the latest brainstorm. These are relatively easily handled. In terms of interruptions, simply set boundaries about when you're not available, or say, "Can we talk about that later?" The Kinetic Kids we've seen are usually very open to that and, in fact, will bound off elsewhere. In terms of projects, always bring it back to the clear objective, assuming you have one, and work toward getting a consensus on whether something will help the project or hurt it. These can definitely be the most fun types of people to work for.

If you work with a Kinetic Kid. In the show *Greater Tuna,* when they're talking about a rambunctious dog, they say, "Throw a glass of iced tea on him and get him to settle." You may feel like that a lot when a colleague is a Kinetic Kid. It's easier to set boundaries here, and preserve the time you need to get your work done. However, particularly if you work in a creative field, this is the person you'll want in your brainstorm session, for the reasons detailed previously. Humor goes a long way with these kids in terms of setting boundaries, and setting structures for when you can interact can be very effective.

The Quiet Kid

The Quiet Kid on the playground. The Quiet Kid is different from the Loner (which we'll talk about shortly). The Quiet Kid will engage in play, have a great time, and be fully engaged. It's just that he or she is not as boisterous as some of the other kids. The Quiet Kid is often the one who comes up with a great idea because he or she has been mulling over the situation and taking it all in. The Quiet Kid tends to balance both types of thinking more readily than other types. He or she is most likely primarily a divergent thinker, but is not likely to share anything until he or she has reached a convergent solution.

The Quiet Kid at work. This is a type that is very comfortable in groups but will rarely present an idea until it's fully fleshed out. This is also a type who in a more kinetic environment might seem to be withdrawn. Nothing could be further from the truth. The Quiet Kid is taking in everything and methodically going through various options. He or she doesn't waste energy, but that doesn't mean this type is intractable. New information is always coming in, and that means adjustments will be made. Quiet Kids tend to be very rational and open to new ideas, even if they don't appear to be swept along by the enthusiasm that sometimes occurs. The Quiet Kid can also have a very calming effect on a work environment, and though it might not seem like it, Quiet Kids and Kinetic Kids complement each other well, and often make a terrific team.

If you work for a Quiet Kid. Don't expect immediate feedback, but when you get it, it will be considered. The Quiet Kid thrives on information that can be put into the data bank, so don't hold back with ideas or solutions. The downside of working for a Quiet Kid is that you may want faster feedback than you'll get. Patience is the watchword when dealing with this type, and the security of knowing that you're never going to get a response that hasn't been considered. Barring other issues, you'll always be free to speak your mind with a Quiet Kid, but try to be more rational than emotional when you can.

If you work with a Quiet Kid. Listen. This is the person who will have considered a lot of issues before speaking. You may not agree, but you'll know that you're not getting a snap judgment. This person may not engage as obviously, but is nonetheless actively engaged. They are observers and thinkers, and as noted, often are great complements to other team members.

The Loner

The Loner on the playground. This is the kid who is happy playing alone. He or she is neither anti-social nor depressed, unless other things are going on. This type simply enjoys being left to his or her own devices. Loners don't necessarily fit one thought process. We have seen Loners who are active, divergent thinkers who are always coming up with great ideas, active play, and those who are more convergent think-ers who can spend hours poring over a model or a drawing. These kids will engage with other kids and participate in group activities, but their preferred type of play is one that is self-sufficient.

The Loner at work. The Loner tends to work best on self-contained projects that require little supervision. In fact, he or she excels at those. We see a lot of coders today who are Loners and who love solving com-plex problems. They may or may not participate in the social aspects of a work environment, but that doesn't mean they don't enjoy them. The Loner is also very dependable and tends to be very detail-oriented. He or she also tends to know when they need help and will ask for it, but for the most part the Loner will have any aspect of a project they're responsible for under control at all times.

If you work for a Loner. Loners tend to be hands-off managers. They'll expect you to come to them with a problem or issue, but because they are used to working on things on their own, they often expect oth-ers to do so as well. This type, however, is seldom seen in senior posi-tions or the C-suite, largely because the need to work with others and be highly public both within and outside an organization.

If you work with a Loner. Respect his or her space. You can count on thoughtful and economical responses to issues and ideas. He or she probably won't enjoy the give-and-take of a dynamic brainstorm-ing meeting, and given a problem that requires a creative solution will prefer to work on it independently. The biggest mistake we see people make, particularly in more active offices, is to assume that Loner wants to be left alone. That's absolutely not true; it's just that his or her first impulse is not to work collaboratively.

The People Pleaser

The People Pleaser on the playground. This is the kid who always wants to fit in and is afraid that he or she doesn't. If you want to get a kid to eat a bug, this is the one to do it. On the positive side, however, this type is always trying to keep things on an even keel. He or she is very sensitive to the dynamics of a group and is expert at making people feel good about themselves. When diverse people need to get along, this is the person you want because he or she is usually an expert listener and able to get people talking. This type also tends to be fairly intuitive about people and has a wealth of observational experience to draw on. The People Pleaser tends to be more of a convergent thinker because he or she is always about acknowledging and validating individuals. This is the overriding goal of this type in its absolute form, though it almost never shows up that way. More likely, being a People Pleaser is a component of a personality that generally has other dominant traits.

The People Pleaser at work. The best part of this type is that the People Pleaser wants to make sure that people get along. He or she is most likely to diffuse conflict by validating each person's position and then seeking to find a middle ground that respects the individuals. This type draws on his or her intuitive skills to complement objective information in any situation. The People Pleaser is, by definition, someone everyone gets along with. However, the mistake people often make in dealing with this type is to assume that he or she is a pushover. Just as the People Pleaser is sensitive to others, he or she is equally sensitive to rules and fairness, and won't just roll over if challenged or taken advantage of.

If you work for a People Pleaser. You'll probably never get yelled at. Don't mistake that for never being corrected or causing anger, however. The People Pleaser will also ask you to consider all sides of an issue before making a decision, just as he or she does. Although this type works hard to ensure that interoffice relationships are peaceful, he or she is not going to avoid conflict when necessary. You probably won't get very far complaining about co-workers or playing politics with this type, either, so if you want validation for that, look elsewhere. The People Pleaser will likely ask you, "Why do you say that?" If really you're looking for a solution, that's great. This type will also provide you with lots of validation and support, even when you're being corrected.

If you work with a People Pleaser. For obvious reasons, these are some of the easiest people to get along with in a work environment. A People Pleaser will listen to you and validate your point of view. Be aware, though, that he or she will also do that for someone you're in conflict with. This type is also great to have on your team because he or she will by their very nature consider the consequences of actions from both business and personal reasons.

~

As stated, no one person is going to fit all these types, but if you take the time to consider the makeup of the people you work for and with, you have a very good chance of working more effectively with them. It's also a good idea to look at yourself in light of these types, and understand your own reactions and behaviors. There is no overt ranking for "plays well with others" in business, but trust me, it's there, and it's as critical as performance in advancing your career.

Ready, Set, Go!

Hopefully by this point, you've at least entertained the idea that play as we've defined and discussed it is to be celebrated and participated in richly. You spent all those years learning how to do it as a kid, and it shaped who you are. Why, as we said at the outset, would you walk away from something that was so critical to making you who you are?

The great thing about this is it only takes jumping in. There are no manuals to read, no courses to take, and so forth. You already know how to do this. If you take nothing else away from this than a willingness to try, then I've done my job. And I want to leave you with a review and recap of the five most important elements of play you can always turn to and that will always be a dependable guide and a great corrective when you go off course, as you inevitably will.

These core principles of play work in business because they are written into our DNA as humans, and we bring that humanity into any situation. In fact, play is our natural state. It is how we remain open to new experiences, express ourselves, and learn. It's about, as we've said, making a choice, seeing where that takes you, and making other choices. Despite the fact that we love to forecast outcomes, results are never truly guaranteed—no matter how much we wish they could be. So our focus must always be on the process rather than the result. Play is that process that offers constant, changing, and surprising opportunities that allow each of us to be our best in whatever you do. Here's what you need to remember.

Make it Up as You Go

We really—none of us—have any idea where all of this is leading. If you allow yourself to consider possibilities, you'll be amazed at what you can come up with. Yes, each choice you make predicates another, and each choice shuts off some options, but the creative process is all about making choices and seeing where they take you. Don't be afraid to go out on a limb, or certainly not in the realm of the imagination. As a friend of mine always says, "You don't go to jail for thinking crazy things. You go to jail for *doing* crazy things." Don't limit your imagination, and even if it takes you far afield, you may end up some place better that you would have thought if you hadn't done that.

Years ago when I was working with Ideal Toys, the company was saddled with a great many porcelain Shirley Temple dolls that hadn't sold. These dolls were slightly more than 2 feet tall, made of extraordinary porcelain, approved by Shirley Temple Black herself, and clothed in the famous Shirley Temple "Stand Up and Cheer" dress. They cost $400 each, which was an extraordinary amount in the early 1980s for a collector doll, and the doll group needed to get rid of the inventory without too much of a loss and without violating the agreements with Shirley Temple Black. The all-important brainstorming session was getting nowhere. Tempers were riding high, and our tiny PR department was in the crosshairs. The problem was, however, as a full year of sales data showed us, and reliable qualitative research, that the market for these dolls was saturated. And our target audience was dying off, literally. Short of slashing the price, which we couldn't do without devaluing all the other collector dolls, we had no idea for new sales.

Finally, as the brand director was hollering and pounding the table, in an admitted fit of pique, I suggested that we use them as skeet and shoot them off the back of the QE2. This prompted many people in the room to laugh, and the head of the doll line to be aghast at the suggestion of ruining "my babies." Most significantly, it changed the outlook in the room from one of hand-wringing to one of possibility. What came out of that, however, was a targeted program of doing targeted, niche marketing which, though commonplace today, was not done then. We got Mrs. Black to sign some dolls and launched a variety of programs. Not all of them were successful, but we solved the problem. By being willing to go "out there," and play in a childlike manner—the way a 10-year-old boy would love to destroy the doll—something productive came out of the play.

A couple of years later, we launched a game called Murder to Go. It was in the mid-1980s, and getting attention for a game during New York Toy Fair was an uphill battle. We took to the streets and spray-painted body outlines on the streets. Completely illegal, of course, and done under cover of night, but it started a conversation. Then, the night before Toy Fair opened, we added "Murder to Go from Ideal" to the outlines around the Toy Center. Of course, we did this without the knowledge of senior management and legal, who would have had to stop us, and we figured that if any members of our team were "caught or killed" they had plausible deniability. And it was all born from another concept steeped in play: better to ask forgiveness than permission.

I'm not advocating breaking the law, of course; what I am suggesting is starting from a mindset where anything is possible. You can always bring your ideas down to earth later, but don't limit the process. And besides, it's fun. Always ask, "What if?"

Tell a Great Story

You can go back Chapter 2 on the importance of story in play, but it bears repeating here that your stories create your reality. Tell a great story, and you'll shape perception, drive purchases, and build success. Children know how to tell stories because they know their audience. They know the buttons to push in talking to parents or teachers. They know how to sway emotion with a good story, and narrative-based play, as noted earlier, is one of the core elements of imaginative engagement.

How you craft your story is critical to your success—whether it's about your career or your business. And the corollary to this is: Don't cede control of your story. Your competitors will try to change your story. Just look at any political campaign in our current culture to see how that happens. Fight for your stories because they define you.

Fail Beautifully

As we discussed earlier, failure is instructive. If you're passionate about what you do, your failures will be instructive. You don't go into something intending to fail; no one in their right mind does that. However, you will fail. I won't minimize the disappointment that comes with failures, but I will say what our coaches used to day: Shake it off. As Frank Coker learned on the way to making an award-winning game, it wasn't the successes that made the game better: It was the failures.

Play to Win

Hopefully this has been implicit in everything that has gone before in this, but the object of playing is to win, and certainly when you're in a competitive situation. I take a very dim view of the recent spate of games for children that are designed to be "co-operative" and for everyone to win. Likewise, when I talk to parents of kids whose grade-school teams don't keep score, I suggest that saving kids from the "pain" of losing only leaves them with the tedium of pointless competition. The world is a competitive place, and teaching kids to play to win and accept that they will sometimes lose is a critical skill. As we noted when we talked about having clear objectives, winning is one of the clearest you can have. Without a benchmark for success, the pleasure of the game is gone. Losing isn't fun, but it also can be an inspiration to try harder, play better, and figure out a way to win. Then, when the win is achieved, it's earned, and it means something.

We do keep score in this world, and it's foolish and unproductive to think otherwise. Humans are by nature competitive, and going for the win—however you define it—and not giving up are what give any endeavor its meaning. Go all in, or what's the point of playing? Things are going to happen—some good, some bad. You can hang out on the sidelines if you want to, but it's more productive and exciting to be part of whatever game you choose to play.

Have Fun

One day many years ago, I was talking to the rector of our church. He had just come from visiting one of our prominent parishioners, who was on her deathbed. The rector was smiling as he talked about her. I asked why he was so happy, as he had just left someone who was going to die very soon.

"As I was leaving," he said, "she grabbed my hand tightly and looked into my eyes, and with the most beautiful smile, she looked at me and said, 'Haven't we had fun?'"

I don't know about how you feel, but from that moment, I've always hoped that when my time comes, I'll be able to say the same thing. I'm not hurrying out of here, but I can say that for the most part that's true. I get to play and make things up virtually every day of my life. I work with amazing people who share the same point of view, and when I fail or get knocked down—which is completely unavoidable—I get back up and start playing again.

We are each responsible for making up our own lives. Why not make up the best possible one? If you don't like things, make up something new, or find the fun in what you've got. Our imaginations—and opposable thumbs—are what make us astonishing creatures. We have an obligation to make the most of the game and create and take responsibility for making it fun.

Now go out and play.

Acknowledgments

I want to thank everyone at Career Press for believing in this project, and my agent, Maryann Karinch, who helped me get this off the ground and whose sense of play is always infectious. Thanks to the hundreds of kids over the years who have let me play with and observe them, and who taught me so much in the process. I also want to thank the people who were so generous with their time in talking to me and playing with the ideas that are in here, including Frank Coker, Stephanie Cota, Jennifer Deare, Bill Doyle, Beth Greenberg, Rick McCabe, Amber Shockey, Steve Sullivan, Wendy Welch, and Ursula Ziegler. Their willingness and the courage to make up their own lives—and literally play them into existence—is consistently inspirational.

Index

A

A Christmas Carol, 86

ADD, 68

Adjustments, 92

Attention Deficit Disorder. See: *ADD.*

Attraction, 159-160

B

Baby Boomers, 14, 78, 82, 88,113

Barad, Jill, 150, 151-152

Barbie, 47, 48, 60, 150, 151, 188, 195

Barrie, James M., 9

Batman, 189

Best Practices, 28

Bettleheim, Bruno, 46-47

Bias Confirmation, 180

Bicycle, 25

Birkin Bag, 31

Boredom, 83

Boundaries, 108

Brainstorming, 116, 203

Brand, 61, 118

"Brand DNA," 55

Bratz, 188

Broadway, 39

Burnout, 96

Burroughs, John, 166

C

C.O.W.S, 53

Candyland, 185

Carnegie, Dale, 30

Catharsis, 34

Chekov, Anton, 63

Chicago (Play), 33

Christmas, 43

Chuck E. Cheese's, 75

Civility, 122, 124, 125

Clarity of Vision, 144

Coding, 149

Coker, Frank, 168, 169

Coleridge, Samuel Taylor, 12

Collaborative Learning, 110

Common Purpose, 110, 111, 118-119, 120-121

Companionship, 109, 110

Confidence, 89

Conflict Scenarios, 104

Constructivism, 95

Convergent Thinking, 116-117, 149

Creativity, 143, 145

D

Danziger, Larry, 26

Dave & Buster's, 76

Deare, Jennifer, 54

Dickens, Charles, 12, 86

Discovery, 38

Divergent Thinking, 116-117, 149

Dix-McCabe, Addie, 76

Don Quixote, 62

Doyle, Bill, 53

Dumbo, 62

E

Easy Bake Oven, 68-70

Edison, Thomas, 179

Eisenhower, Dwight D, 13

Engagement, 67

Equilibration, 95

Exit Strategy, 182

F

Facebook, 65, 67

Failure, 38, 170, 177, 208

Fear, 153-154

Fear, 16-17, 175, 177

Fisher-Price, 129

Fluidity, 179

Focus Groups, 180

FOMO, 96-97

Franklin, Benjamin, 126

Free-Range Kids, 82

Freud, Sigmund, 48

Fritos, 190

G

Gender Differentiation, 129-131

Generation X, 78

Genius, 150, 152

Germany, 13-14

GI Joe, 189

Gladwell, Malcolm, 32-33

Global Positioning System.
See: *GPS*.

GPS, 90

Great Depression, 13

Greater Tuna, 201

Group Dynamics, 85, 87, 110, 117, 126-127, 142-143

Group Play, 103, 104, 106-107, 109, 111, 114

H

Hamlet, 57, 173

Harry Potter, 24, 46, 53, 57, 62, 111, 189

Harvard Business School, 155

Hasbro, 68-69

Henry the V, 46, 52

Hierarchies, 108

Hiring, 160-161, 162

Holiday Hills, 13

Hot Wheels, 16

I

Ideal Toys, 206-207

Imagination, 87-88, 89, 165, 193, 195, 206-207

Indiana Jones, 58

Information Overload, 94, 100

Information Processing, 94, 99-100

Innovation, 143, 158

Interaction, 107, 108, 111

Intuition, 145-146, 147-148, 150

iPad, 26-27, 150, 176

J

Jason Bourne, 58

Jeep, 191

Jobs, Steve, 27, 150

K

Kermit the Frog, 24

Kinetic, 29

Kraus-D'Isa, Linda, 90

L

LEGO, 10, 22, 36, 65, 140, 144, 152

Lego Movie, The, 152

Level of Development, 26

Levitin, Daniel J., 75

LinkedIn, 161-162

Lions, 97

Litzky, Michele, 135

M

Macy, R.H., 44

Mad Men, 123, 199

Man from U.N.C.L.E, The, 88

Manners, 122

Mary Poppins, 185

Massive Multi-Player Online Games. See: *MMOGs.*

Millenials, 79

MMOGs, 168-169

Modernizing, 86

Monopoly, 189

Montessori, 25

Much Ado About Nothing, 46

Muscle Memory, 25

N

Nerf, 78

Network, 109

Neural Pathways, 26

New York Toy Fair, 207

Next Empire, The, 168

O

Objectives, 11

Organized Mind, The, 75

P

PBM, 168-169

Peter Pan, 9, 10, 12, 19

Pezzano, Linda, 186

PF Flyers, 62

Piaget, 25, 139

Piaget, Jean, 95

Pictionary, 186, 187

Play, 10, 18, 21-22, 35-36,

  Accommodation in, 95

  Active Process of, 140

  Alone, 81, 84, 94

  Assimilation in, 95

  Associative, 104, 106

  Attention and, 74

  Boredom and, 83

  Brands in, 61

  Creativity in, 143

  Experiences in, 88, 196

  Experimentation in, 91

  Exploration in, 88, 91

  Expression in, 88

  Imagination in, 88, 89, 206-207

  In Groups, 103

  Interaction in, 107

  Learning in, 38

  Playmates and, 159

  Principles in, 193

  Productivity in, 195

  Reasons for Working, 28

Recreation vs, 73

Re-examination and, 193

Role Play in, 56

Self Reliance and, 91

Stories in, 47, 49, 66, 67, 71, 208

Playgroup, 82

Playground Types, 197

  Bossy, 198-199

  Kinetic, 200-201

  Loner, 201, 202-203

  People-Pleaser, 203-204

  Quiet, 201-202

Play By Mail. See: *PBM.*

Play-Doh, 76

Pokemon, 112-113

Power Point, 24, 155

R

Rainbow Connection, The, 24

Rainbow Loom, 66

Ratey, John J., 76

Reactions, 92

Reagan, Ronald, 147

Reality, 51

Recess, 75

Recreation, 73, 76-78

Red Bull, 63, 65, 79

Repetitive Activity, 26

Research, 181

Response, 92, 93

Retailing, 157-158

Risk (Board Game), 185

Risk, 17, 141-142, 153,
155-156, 166

Robbins, Tony, 35

Roberts, Julia, 116, 130, 131-132

Smartphone, 96

Social Media, 64-65, 96, 161, 192

Socializing, 81, 104

Spider-Man, 23

St. Paul, 22

Stakes, 59

Stories, 43, 45-46, 49, 71
Structure of, 51

Stress, 39, 97-98

Superman, 51

S

Sandberg, Sheryl, 30

Santa Claus, 43

Scrooge, Ebenezer, 86-87

Self-reliance, 90, 93

Sex, Lies & Creativity, 116, 130

Sexism, 134

Shakespeare, William, 9, 14, 46,
52, 57, 173, 197

Share, 105-106

Shirley Temple Black, 206-207

Shockey, Amber, 161, 163, 166

Skateboard, 141

Skateboarding, 57-58

Skenazy, Lenore, 82

T

Tasks, 11

Teenage Mutant Ninja Turtles, 60

"10,000 Hours of Practice," 27

Thinking Processes, 115

Three Stooges, The, 131

Tickle Me Elmo, 187

Tide Detergent, 61

Tipping Point, The, 32

Tolkien, J.R.R, 62

Trivial Pursuit, 186

Turing, Alan, 150

Twelfth Night, 14, 46

Twitter, 65

U

United States, 12-13

Uses of Enchantment, The, 46

V

Viet Nam, 14

W

Where the Wild Things Are, 109

Wizard of Oz, The, 53, 57

Wolf of Wall Street, The, 136

World War I, 12

World War II, 12-13, 191

Y

Youtube, 65, 66, 120

Z

Ziglar, Zig, 141

About the Author

Chris Byrne is a 30-plus-year veteran of the toy industry and is considered one of the leading experts on the business in the United States. In addition to his consultancy, Byrne Communications, Inc., he is a partner in aNb Media and content director for TTPM (TimetoPlayMag.com). During his career, he has held a variety of positions with toy companies covering marketing, media, operations, product development, and creative. In 1988, he formed New York–based Byrne Communications. He is a researcher, analyst, and consultant who has worked with a variety of Fortune 100 companies tracking kid trends, product development, and strategic marketing campaigns. In addition to marketing development, Byrne has created and implemented programs to facilitate creative thinking, brainstorming, and employee training. He speaks regularly at conferences and for companies on the power of play in fostering innovation.

Byrne Communications has consulted to a wide variety of toy and entertainment companies, crafting and implementing research studies, marketing plans, product development strategies, personnel training, and more, helping them to effectively understand markets and consumer behavior. Byrne Communications has helped in the development of successful product lines—hard goods and soft goods, promotional items, and so forth—for new and established IP. Byrne Communications has also developed strategic marketing programs in the financial, food, consumer packaged goods, and beverage industries.

Byrne is widely published on the topic of toys, marketing, and family life, and in addition to his work with Time to Play he is editor-at-large for the trade publications *Toys & Family Entertainment* and *Royalties*. He is also a contributing blogger for *The Huffington Post*. His book *Toy Time* was published by the Three Rivers imprint of Random House in 2013, and *Serious Fun: An Introduction to the U.S. Toy Industry* was published by Business Experts Press in early 2014.

In addition, Byrne is widely quoted in the media and appears regularly on local and national television commenting on toys, demonstrating new products and business, and business practices. He has appeared on *Live! With Kelly & Michael, Oprah, Soap Talk, Today, Good Morning America, The CBS Evening News, ABC Nightly News,* FOX News, *CBS This Morning, Good Day New York, CNBC, CNN, MSNBC, ABC, The Motley Fool,* National Public Radio, and Bloomberg Television and Radio, and on countless other national and local market business and consumer programs around the country and internationally.